AN INTRODUCTION TO
ANTHROPOLOGY

AN INTRODUCTION TO
ANTHROPOLOGY

SIMON COLEMAN AND HELEN WATSON

CHARTWELL
BOOKS, INC.

A QUINTET BOOK

Published by Chartwell Books
A Division of Book Sales, Inc.
110 Enterprise Avenue
Secaucus, New Jersey 07094

ISBN 1-55521-574-2

This book was designed and produced by
Quintet Publishing Limited
6 Blundell Street
London N7 9BH

CREATIVE DIRECTOR: Peter Bridgewater
PROJECT EDITOR: Caroline Beattie
EDITOR: Susan Baker
PICTURE RESEARCHER: Liz Eddison

Typeset in Great Britain by
Central Southern Typesetters, Eastbourne
Manufactured in Hong Kong by
Regent Publishing Services Limited
Printed in Hong Kong by
Leefung-Asco Printers Limited

CONTENTS

CHAPTER ONE

THE MEANING

OF ANTHROPOLOGY

As human beings we are reassured by living in a familiar environment. In our every-day lives, we are surrounded by objects, people and buildings that are well known to us and which we think we can understand. What would happen, however, if we were suddenly transported hundreds or thousands of miles across the world into a new social setting, and were surrounded by people who spoke a different language, ate unfamiliar food and had never heard of our country of origin? Instead of being confident members of our own society, we would become like children, constantly needing to ask questions, and striving to comprehend the confusing range of activities around us. In our effort to reach some kind of viable interpretation of our new environment, we would be both intellectually stimulated and emotionally drained. The situation would also require constant vigilance to catch the nuances of a language that we only half understood, and to avoid committing a socially unacceptable action that would have seemed entirely reasonable in our own society.

THE STUDY OF
HUMANKIND...

These are some of the problems faced by anthropologists as they carry out their work. On the one hand, as scholars, they must try to comprehend and record such things as the myths, rituals, economic systems, family pat-

LEFT *The human experience of fieldwork. Anthropologists often form close personal friendships with local people during fieldwork: an anthropologist in the field, Siberut Island, Indonesia.*

terns and forms of political organization of a given society or group. They must attempt to translate their experiences of immersion in another society into a permanent record, such as a book or a film, which can present their understanding to a remote audience or readership. On the other hand, as human beings, they are likely to form close friendships with many of those whom they meet 'in the field'. Thus anthropology has elements of art and science, humanistic interpretation and systematic recording. Hortense Powdermaker, an American anthropologist, has noted that an anthropologist is both 'stranger and friend' to those whom he or she studies – a participant in their lives for a year or more, but also a partly detached observer of their society.

OPPOSITE *A Girahya woman dressed in fine clothes for the annual Gangaur fair. The 'imported additions' to her elaborate costume include sunglasses and junk jewellery.*

7

Before we go any further, we need to make clear what we mean by the term 'anthropology'. It derives from two Greek words: *anthropos* meaning humankind, and *logos* meaning word, or study. Thus, in its broadest sense, anthropology refers to the study of human beings and societies, both alive and dead, flourishing or extinct. In practice, the term includes a number of distinct but related sub-fields, which have developed their own theoretical and methodological specializations over the past century. These can be summarized as follows:

PHYSICAL ANTHROPOLOGY

This has close connections to natural sciences like biology and genetics. It is concerned to understand the way humans have evolved from their *hominid* ancestors over the last few million years, as well as the extent to which we share genetic characteristics with other primates such as the great apes, gorillas and chimpanzees. Palaeoanthropologists examine fossil remains of extinct primates. Meanwhile, those *physical anthropologists* concerned with the science of *ethology* study the behaviour of animals in their natural settings. Some scholars are also interested in looking at human variation – the physical differences between peoples adapted to different environments.

ARCHAEOLOGY

Archaeologists examine the many different forms of social organization and culture that have characterized humankind through time. They recover data by excavating sites of past human habitation and meticulously recording the objects, settlement patterns and remains of the people whose lives they are trying to understand. American scholars in particular regard this discipline as a form of anthropology.

ANTHROPOLOGICAL LINGUISTICS

Language, as a highly complex means of communication used by humans throughout the world, is a rich subject of study. As well as being interested in comparing language forms, some anthropologists are also concerned to understand what the use of language in a given context can say about the social or political relations amongst the people being studied. As we shall see, others, like the French anthropologist Claude Lévi-Strauss, have tried to use insights derived from linguistics to understand the way people think about the world they live in.

SOCIAL AND CULTURAL ANTHROPOLOGY

This involves the study of the culture and social organization of living peoples. It is related to the practice of *ethnology,* which is often defined as the comparative study of cultures. In the past, the work of anthropologists was distinguished from that of sociologists because the former usually focussed on non-industrialized peoples, while the latter concentrated more explicitly on their own western societies. More recently, however, the gap has narrowed, as anthropologists have begun to apply their research methods to industrial societies, including

LEFT *The process of immersion in another society and culture often calls for adjustment to a different way of life in unfamiliar surroundings: the potters' quarter and rubbish dump settlement in Cairo. It is estimated that five thousand people live in these districts where the air is thick with smoke from the kilns and fires.*

their own, and sociologists have expanded their interests beyond Europe and North America. However, while sociologists are usually more concerned to examine and analyse general trends in society, often using statistical methods, anthropologists put an emphasis on the close and detailed study of particular communities or sub-cultures. Thus they usually work by engaging in *participant observation*. This means that they live with the people whom they study, sometimes for a period of years, and try to understand the way a society works from the point of view of a member born into the community. *Ethnography* is the term used to describe the process of recording and analyzing data gleaned from observation.

The various sub-disciplines of anthropology outlined above should not be seen as mutually exclusive. For instance, the study of *ethno-archaeology* investigates the use, in the present, of *material culture,* and tries to use such research to form hypotheses about social life in the past. In addition, the discipline is developing all the time as the world itself changes. Many new and fascinating areas of interest are emerging, including medical anthropology, historical anthropology, feminist anthropology, to name but a few of them.

BELOW *Anthropologists have been interested in the genetic characteristics humans share with other primates. The London Sketch Book's cartoon of Charles Darwin and a curious ape-man in 1874.*

RIGHT *Hunters and the hunted: a scene from the life of prehistoric peoples shown in a cave painting in the Matopo Hills, Zimbabwe.*

LEFT *Few people remain isolated from the products of modern technology and industrialization. A Dogon man carries a motorbike through the alleys of his village.*

RIGHT *Art or culture? A Sikh bride's hands are decorated with intricate designs painted with henna paste. There is a very similar custom among Bedouins and Muslim communities in the Middle East and North Africa.*

BOTTOM RIGHT *Kumar: the virgin goddess of the Kathmandu Valley. At the annual festival of Indra Jatra, the people of Kathmandu celebrate and give thanks for the protection of the goddess. Kumar is wheeled around the capital city in a golden chariot.*

THE IMPORTANCE OF CULTURE

Before we go further, it is worth discussing a concept which is key to the study of anthropology as a whole: *culture*. Think, for a moment, about how we use the word in everyday language. *'Material culture'* refers to the objects we possess or perhaps covet, and it is this which forms much of the subject-matter of archaeology. On the other hand, if someone is called 'cultured' this is usually taken to mean that they are refined and well-educated, and therefore identifies the word with the artistic and academic worlds. If anthropologists were simply to study the latter kind of culture, the subject would become a branch of art history. Much more broadly, we use phrases like 'American' or 'British' culture in very imprecise ways, pointing out what we think are characteristic values and practices of a given country.

In fact, the meaning of 'culture' has long been debated by social and cultural anthropologists. In the 1950s, two American scholars, Kroeber

and Kluckhohn, found over 150 definitions of the term in academic literature! One definition that proved to be influential was that made by the early English anthropologist, Sir Edward Burnett Tylor (1832–1917). The first lines of his book *Primitive Culture* (1871) state:

'Culture or civilization, taken in its wide ethnographic sense, is that complex whole which includes knowledge, belief, art, moral law, custom, and any other capabilities and habits acquired by man as a member of society.'

Although many anthropologists would now disagree with parts of this definition, it emphasizes some points that are widely accepted. Culture in a broad sense may be thought of as knowledge and values that are passed on from generation to generation in a social group. Some cultural knowledge, such as ways of measuring time, are likely to be widely known within a given group, while other forms of knowledge, such as particular myths or legends, may be less widely shared. Since culture has an effect on the way people think, it can also have

BELOW *Spearing fish in the southern Sudan, a traditional fishing technique of the Dinka tribe. Fathers teach their sons the skills of spearmaking, and from an early age boys practice to acquire the speed and balance fishspearing requires.*

RIGHT *The cultural definition of social roles is often most obvious in the case of gender. These Nubian girls (aged 11 and 13) from a strict Muslim community are in semi-seclusion, confined to the home unless in the company of a chaperone or male guardian. By contrast, their younger brother is free to play outside.*

some influence on behaviour. However, unlike the genetic characteristics of humankind, it is passed on through social rather than biological means.

For the purposes of description, anthropologists tend to talk about a given culture as if it were a static, clearly defined, unchanging entity. It is important to realize, however, that cultural knowledge is in fact very diffuse, subject to external influences and the multiple interpretations of its inheritors. A given individual may even be subject to the influences of two cultures simultaneously. Gypsies, for instance, combine a knowledge of their own ways of life and beliefs with an awareness of those of the wider societies in which they live.

American students of contemporary societies often call themselves cultural anthropologists. They emphasize the need to focus on the rules of culture, the common codes and meanings which allow members of a community to understand each other and cooperate successfully. Sometimes, they also regard cultural anthropology as dealing with virtually all the non-biological aspects of life. British scholars, who usually call themselves social anthropologists, have focussed on the observable social relations in a given community – the ways in which people are organized into social groups and allotted roles. In recent years, however, these differences in interest between the two approaches have tended to become blurred.

BELOW Community cooperation in Nogueira, Amazonia. Ajuri work parties are formed to clear areas for the planting of manioc gardens. After work the owner of the land provides a meal for the invited participants. People who are unable to join the Ajuri either send someone in their place or remain in debt until the next agricultural season.

RIGHT *How people meet their food needs is one basic question in anthropological research. Fishing in Malawi, a man casts his net in Elephant Marsh.*

BELOW *The meeting of Amazonian Indians in Altamira. The meeting attracted the attention and support of the international community challenging the construction of a massive dam and the inevitable destruction of the Indians' land and way of life in the name of national development.*

THE IMPORTANCE OF ANTHROPOLOGY

This book will focus on the branch of the discipline we have defined as social and cultural anthropology. Thus, when we use the word anthropology in the future, we will be referring to this branch of the subject. Our aims are twofold: first, to introduce the reader to anthropology as it is practised, particularly in Britain and the United States; and second to give an idea of its moral and intellectual relevance to life in contemporary society. We shall concentrate on its historical development, its ways of gathering and analyzing information, some of its leading practitioners and some examples of anthropological fieldwork and analysis.

The American scholar George Stocking has written:

'If all disciplines ultimately originate in and return to questions of general human concern, this is especially so in the case of anthropology, where the nature of humankind is at issue' (1987: 324).

We hope to show that anthropology raises some fascinating questions and provides some stimulating answers:

– How can we understand the concepts, values and modes of thought of people who live in societies apparently so different from our own?

– How does the understanding of another culture or sub-culture help us to understand the way we ourselves perceive the world and relate to others?

– Is it possible to construct general laws of human behaviour?

Anthropology is a vibrant and developing subject, which provides intellectual stimulation as well as much valuable information for development workers, aid organizations and policy makers throughout the world. In a world where cultural interaction is increasing all the time, we cannot afford to ignore the insights anthropology provides us with.

ABOVE *Many anthropologists are interested in the form and content of ritual activity. The week before Easter is marked by daily processions of life-sized statues of Jesus and Mary in Andalusia. Each statue is owned by a different Brotherhood.*

CHAPTER TWO

THE MAKING
OF ANTHROPOLOGY

STUDENTS who enrol on an anthropology course in a modern university department are likely to spend much of their first few weeks in a state of confusing but exciting disorientation. In a single day, they might go to a lecture on peasant economies in eastern Europe, before hurrying to a seminar on Hinduism in India, or perhaps writing an essay on marriage payments within the Nuer tribe of Sudan. The *ethnographers* of today work throughout the globe, in rural and urban, remote and easily accessible settings. They are interested in the political, economic, religious and reproductive practices of the peoples whom they study.

Anthropology has emerged out of a highly complex series of developments, and nowadays encompasses a vast range of interests and specializations. We are going to look at a few of these in order to understand how it has acquired some of its present interests.

EARLY ENCOUNTERS...

In one sense, the practice of anthropology started as soon as people began to reflect upon their own society and beliefs, and decided consciously to compare them with other societies with which they came into contact. The Greek historian Herodotus (*c 484–425 BC*) spent many years travelling in Asia, Egypt and Greece, and wrote detailed descriptions of the dress, crops, etiquette and rituals of the people he encountered. Ibn Khaldun (1332–1406) was a politician and

historian who lived in Algeria for many years. He produced a remarkable piece of scholarship, contrasting what he saw as two types of society, the supposedly wild, aggressive and nomadic Bedouins, and the sedentary, cultivated and sometimes corrupt city-dwellers, who depended on local agriculture for their existence.

Both of these men were prompted by the experience of meeting societies other than their own to reflect upon the different customs they witnessed, and to express their thoughts in writing in order to inform others. Similarly, from the Middle Ages onwards, European explorers, sailors and missionaries increasingly

ABOVE *The women's festival of Tij where women fast and bathe in the sacred Bagmati river in the temple of Pashupathinath, Kathmandu. The purpose of the ritual is to purify the body and soul and to secure a happy and productive marriage.*

OPPOSITE *Girahya women returning home with earthen pots of buttermilk from a nearby village.*

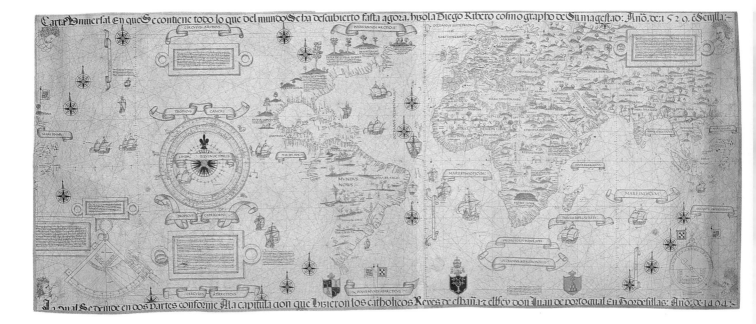

ABOVE *A 16th century view of the world. Diego Ribero's World Map of 1529.*

began to report home with stories of the new lands and customs they had seen. As early as the 13th century, Marco Polo was writing accounts of the Chinese court to his relatives in Italy.

From at least the 15th century, with the fitting out of great voyages of discovery and conquest, considerable debate arose concerning the nature and customs of the 'savages' described by sailors and traders. This was encouraged by the new invention of printing, which rapidly spread travellers' tales amongst literate sections of the population.

Late in the 16th century, the French essayist Michel de Montaigne (1533–92) combined his reading of classical authors such as Xenophon, Lucretius and Virgil with his knowledge of the explorations of the New World. He tried to reject the purely pejorative implications of words like 'barbaric' or 'savage', and attempted to understand the morality of other peoples on their own terms. Montaigne's early form of *cultural relativism* was rare in an era still dominated by the biblical account of the origins of humankind. Often, controversy centred around the issue of whether people with a different coloured skin could be considered as fellow descendants of Adam. The 'discovery' of America led in the 16th century to debates about the nature of the

Indians encountered. Were they rational, human beings – in other words, like Europeans – or did they, like animals, belong to a different order of existence?

Many saw them not merely as remote in space from Europe, but also remote in time. They were perceived as the remnants of humanity at its origins, before parts of it had progressed into the civilizations of Europe. What is clear from many early scholarly discussions of 'exotic' countries and peoples is that they were written by people who had never actually journeyed far beyond the shores of their own European lands. Information came from the accounts of travellers and explorers, or sometimes in the form of answers to lists of questions which scholars sent out with expeditions to distant countries.

Philosophers and social theorists could use the notion of 'uncivilized humanity' to make general points about human nature or their own societies through speculation and abstract reasoning rather than a close examination of evidence from other societies.

Writing in 1651, the Englishman Thomas Hobbes (1588–1679) suggested that humankind in its 'natural' state, without political organization, was inherently selfish and violent. He regarded the American Indians as close to this

LEFT *The nomadic peoples of North Africa have had a long history of contact with settled communities. A Berber couple in western clothes outside the traditional black tent of the Berber people in Sidi Ali of the Middle Atlas region, Morocco.*

RIGHT *William Hodges'*
painting displays the common
stereotypes of his day.
Cautious Landing at Tanna
shows the brave sailor-
explorers confronting the
savages of the New Hebrides.

BELOW *A contemporary*
illustration of
the western image of the
'noble savage'. An Ethiopian
nomad, now armed with a
rifle, stands guard over the
desert waterhole below him in
a deep volcanic crater.

LEFT *An incised drawing from
the upper Palaeolithic period
shows a ritual dance – a rare
record of social and religious
activity in the 7th millenium
BC. The Grotta di Addaura,
near Palermo, Sicily.*

level of existence, where peoples' lives were
supposedly 'poor, nasty, brutish and short'.
The opposite point of view was presented in
much of the work of Jean-Jacques Rousseau
(1712–78), who linked happiness to life in a state
of nature, free from the corrupting influences of
sophistication and civilization. This view had
some parallels with the biblical idea of a pristine
state of humankind before its fall from grace.

Rousseau was writing in the Age of the En-
lightenment, a time when human progress was
seen to be based on the growth of rationality
and increasing knowledge which could displace
older, superstitious beliefs. Thus few shared his
view that civilization might actually have entered
a downward spiral of corruption and degenera-
tion. Rather, a number of ideas began to emerge

which were to be important for the later development of anthropology as a full academic
discipline. These included a new confidence in
the ability of the natural sciences to reveal much
about the workings of the world, as well as the
idea of progress.

During the Middle Ages, the plants and
animals of the world were perceived to be ranked
in a static order, created by God, called the *Chain
of Being*. By the 17th and 18th centuries the
'Chain' was sometimes seen in more dynamic
terms, as involving a form of ladder whereby
the higher forms had ascended through time
out of the condition of the lower forms. Thus
cultures could be ranked in terms of progress,
with European society as the acme of development – both morally and culturally.

RIGHT *A 19th century photograph by James Mooney showing part of the Ghost Dance of the Arapaho Indians. The North American Indians' Ghost Dance cults stressed the need to return to Indian ways of life which were breaking down. The Indians believed that if the traditional patterns of life were restored, the buffaloes (being slaughtered by white settlers) would return and the dead ancestors would come back to defend them. The Ghost Dances were believed to be a way of driving the whites out of Indian territories by giving the Indians magical protection against the settlers' bullets.*

ANTHROPOLOGY BECOMES A DISCIPLINE

Anthropology became an academic subject in its own right in the 19th century. 'Ethnological' institutions and societies began to emerge in Europe and America, devoted largely to the study of the physical, linguistic and cultural characteristics of 'non-civilized' peoples. Sir Edward Tylor became a Reader in anthropology in Oxford in 1884, and in 1888 departments were started at Harvard and Clark Universities in America.

Colonialism and missionary work encouraged Europeans to continue to expand into Australia, Africa, Latin America, Melanesia, and India. The study of indigenous peoples could often be justified on the grounds that colonial administrators could learn better how to educate and control those under their charge. In North America, the fate of the Indians at the hands of white settlers became a burning issue of the day. It was regarded as important to collect as much information on them as possible before they died out, were exterminated or became a part of 'civilized' society. John Powell had conducted geological field trips in Colorado River country, and was convinced that stereotypes of Indians as ignorant and violent were misleading. He persuaded the American Congress to set up the Bureau of American Ethnology in 1879. This was aimed at providing information on Indian groups that could be used to help them assimilate into the rest of American society peacefully.

During most of the 19th century, the exact status of anthropology was ambiguous. It encompassed anything from the measuring of

LEFT *A 12th-century bronze sculpture from Nigeria of a man's head showing the pattern of his decorative tribal scarifications.*

RIGHT *Maasai warriors,
Kenya. Moving beyond
appearances, modern
anthropologists are more
interested in social
organization and everyday
activities in other cultures
than in the images conjured up
by tribal costume.*

RIGHT *A traditional herbalist
doctor-healer surrounded by
his medical notes and books of
prescriptions in the south west
province of Cameroon.*

the shapes and sizes of heads to the collecting of artefacts to fill the museums of European university towns. Its connections with the natural sciences, especially zoology and biology, were still close, and this can still be seen today in the Pitt-Rivers Museum in Oxford. Here, ethnological material, in line with the 19th-century charter of the museum, is still classified into *typological* groups in the same manner as vegetable and animal species. Such an organization was congenial to those who saw anthropology as a natural science of humankind devoted to the comparative study of races.

In 1898, an expedition was sent out to the Torres Straits from Cambridge University in England which embodied both the interests of the 19th century and those of the anthropology of the future. It was led by Alfred Haddon, a museum curator, zoologist and expert in tropical fauna, and was prompted by his concern at the apparent disappearance of the customs of peoples in Melanesia. He took physical measurements of natives, recorded local customs and studied art; Rivers, a psychologist, collected sociological data and worked on studying the visual perception of the islanders; others worked on hearing, smell, native medicine, and linguistics. Artefacts and skulls were collected.

The expedition was noteworthy because it involved trained specialists working in the field, gathering information which was recorded as meticulously as possible. One important result was the method Rivers perfected for collecting genealogies of individuals – their ties to their parents, children, grandparents, and so on. He thus provided important early work on the study of *kinship,* a field of inquiry which one anthropologist has described as being as important for anthropology as 'logic is to philosophy or the nude is to art' (Fox, 1967: 10). Haddon was later to remark:

'One of the things of which I am most proud in a somewhat long life is that I was the means of seducing Rivers from the path of virtue . . . into that of anthropology' (quoted in Quiggens, 1942: 97).

ABOVE *A man in a garden plot in Western Samoa with his hoe and umbrella.*

ABOVE *A gathering of Tasmanian aborigines painted in 1859 by Robert Dowling. The expressions and poses illustrate the common 19th-century view of primitive people – lazy, uncivilized and brutish. The painting depicts the 'savagery' of the group itself by the aggressive stance of the spear carriers and the snarling figure on the right of the picture.*

THE IDEA OF EVOLUTION

George Stocking, an American historian of anthropology, has described the attitude of many Victorian Britons to non-European peoples in the following way:

'. . . while the relative position of different savage peoples was a matter of debate . . . the general characteristics of savages were clear enough. Dark-skinned and small of stature, unattractive, unclothed and unclean, promiscuous and brutal with their women, they worshipped the spirits animating animals or even sticks and stones . . .' (1987: 234–5).

Significantly, the image presented is that of a person who is not only geographically remote, but also the exact opposite of the ideal Victorian gentleman: white, attractive, clean (this virtue was, after all, next to godliness), faithful to a single wife, and the worshipper of a single God. Implicit in the image is the notion of *cultural evolution,* an idea which achieved the status of a dominant theory in the 19th century. Scholars began to seek scientific rather than theological explanations for the differences in development between countries of western civilization and what were perceived as technologically and culturally more primitive societies.

The idea of evolution was encouraged by the work of a number of disciplines. Geological evidence suggested that the earth was much older than the Bible suggested, while archaeological discoveries such as implements recovered from Danish peat bogs were taken to confirm the theory that humanity had gone through sequential ages of stone, bronze and iron.

In 1859, Charles Darwin (1809–82) published *On the Origin of Species,* the first formal statement of the theory of evolution by 'natural selection'. This suggested that organisms were in competition with forces of nature, and those best able to survive did so at a higher rate and passed on their advantageous characteristics to others through genetic transmission. Darwin's theory was phrased in terms of gradual change rather than discrete stages of evolution, and did not imply the idea of progress in a single direction. Nor was it intended to apply to the development of society. However, the cultural evolutionists had rather different ideas. The English philosopher Herbert Spencer (1820–1903), for instance, stated that all living things, including societies and institutions, could be ranked on a single scale, ranging from the most simple to the most complex.

The basic idea of *cultural evolutionism* was that society and culture had developed in a regular series of predictable stages. Scholars hoped to develop a science whereby universal laws of human behaviour could explain the stages of development. Contemporary 'primitive' cultures were regarded as paralleling earlier stages through which European cultures, the high points of cultural development, had reached.

In fact, the evolutionists had varied interests and backgrounds, as well as different attitudes to the 'primitives'. Sir James Frazer (1854–1941), a Cambridge classicist who became the first Professor of Anthropology of Liverpool University in 1908, lived in a world surrounded by books. He became famous through his authorship of *The Golden Bough,* (published in 13 volumes from 1890 on). This was a tremendous but highly speculative work of scholarship, comparing customs and beliefs from through-

LEFT *Charles Darwin, 1809–82, author of* On the Origin of Species.

LEFT *The massive stone Buddha at the ancient site of Polonnoruwa, Sri Lanka.*

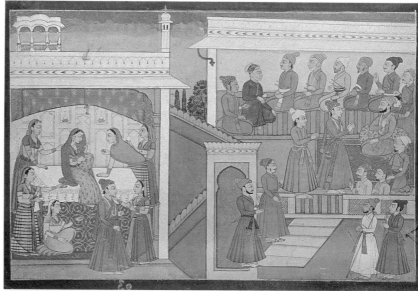

ABOVE *A massive Olmec carved stone head, Mexico. The rise of Olmec civilization began as early as 1500 BC.*

ABOVE RIGHT *An elaborate artistic record of the wedding of Nala and Damayanti from Bilas Pur, India. The manuscript (1750) shows the Lady Damayanti waiting in the bedroom (left) while her husband Nala (right) greets his new father-in-law.*

RIGHT *The modern and ancient world exist side-by-side for people in many cultures. This Egyptian village near the Valley of the Kings lies across the Nile from modern-day Luxor. Some villagers keep their crops and goats in the pharonic temples.*

out the world in an attempt to trace the evolution of religion in human society. Anthropological legend states that, when asked if he would like to visit or meet any of the peoples about whom he wrote, he exclaimed in horror: 'God forbid!'

Others had had direct experience of societies very different from their own. Tylor, for instance, spent a year travelling in the United States, Canada and Mexico, and believed that the human mind was the same in all human cultures, although the stages of cultural development varied.

The American lawyer, Lewis Henry Morgan (1818–81), was one of the most important and influential of the evolutionists, not least because of his book, *Ancient Society,* published in 1877. Much of his interest came from his contact with Iroquois Indians of New York State. His enthusiasm even led him to found a secret society, called 'The Gordion Knot', which held meetings at night, around campfires, in authentic Indian costume. While concerned with legal themes, such as kinship terms, family, government and property, he also constructed an all-embracing theory of evolution in which 'the lines of human progress' were seen to have developed in three stages – from savagery, to barbarism, to civilization.

A key factor in the schema was the development of technology. Barbarism was believed to emerge with the development of pottery, and civilization with the use of an alphabet and writing. The stages were also associated with the increasing importance of property and advances in morals, since he suggested (on no real evidence) that in early societies sexual promiscuity was customary. A similar idea was put forward by the Scottish jurist John McLennan, (1827–81).

An evolutionary position which has had a major and long-term influence on western society was that originally developed by Karl Marx (1818–83). He attempted to show that new forms of society inevitably emerged as individuals and groups struggled to gain access to and control over the production, use and ownership of material goods. Marx's colleague, Friedrich Engels (1820–95), supported Morgan's work in America on the origin of the family. Through Engels, Morgan was to become an important figure in the work of Soviet social scientists.

BELOW LEFT *The remains of the Neolithic village of Skara Brae in Orkney, Scotland. Stone 'furniture' can be identified in the interior of the house – a dresser by the far wall, beds on the right and left and a hearth in the centre.*

BELOW *Ritual activity is considered to be one of the universal aspects of human social life. A man from the Girahya tribe carrying a clay horse to be sacrificed to Bhakar Baosi, the mountain God, on the 'event of a fulfilled desire'. In this culturally diverse part of India he has bought the horse from a potter in a nearby multi-caste village.*

RIGHT *The 'other side' of primitive art. A tribal image from Nigeria of encounters with the barbaric white men. The sculpture represents a Portuguese invader.*

OPPOSITE, TOP The Death of Cook *painted by John Cleveley. Polynesian islanders considered that Captain Cook represented the year-God Lono. Cook participated in ceremonies to renew the fertility of the land while priests made the customary offerings to Lono. He was killed by one of the islanders in 1779.*

RIGHT *Anthropological research reveals the complex practices and purposes of ritual activity in different cultures. An Oboo or ritual cairn in Hulun Buir, Inner Mongolia. Regular ceremonies are held here to honour the spirits of the lineage ancestors. During rituals at the Oboo, offerings of food and alcohol are made, 'wind horse' flags are attached, and the cairn is circled clockwise on horseback.*

THE END OF REVELRY... REACTIONS AGAINST CULTURAL EVOLUTIONISM

In 1896, the anthropologist Franz Boas (1858–1942) published a paper called *The Limitations of the Comparative Method of Anthropology*. The last two lines of this stated: 'Up to this time we have too much reveled in more or less ingenious vagaries. The solid work is still all before us'. The revelry to which he referred was that of many of the evolutionists, whose research he saw as inherently racist and founded on very little evidence.

Boas' polemics against the evolutionists and his alternative method of practising anthropology were to prove highly influential within American anthropology. He was born and brought up in Germany, the son of a successful businessman, and trained originally in physics, maths and geography. Like many early anthropologists, he entered the subject almost by accident, since he was 'converted' to ethnography during a field trip among Arctic Eskimos that was intended to investigate the properties of seawater!

It is possible that, as a German of Jewish descent who came to settle in the United States, he was especially sensitive to the more excessively *ethnocentric* claims of cultural evolutionism, which seemed to treat the white Anglo-Saxon male as the peak of spiritual, physical and cultural development. For Boas, all cultures were equal but different, and the attempt to classify them according to a predetermined evolutionary schema was not only insulting to their separate historical developments, but also bad scholarship. Instead, the scholar had to use a variety of complex techniques to understand how a given group had developed. These included using archaeological evidence, the mapping out of the diffusion of cultural traits amongst neighbouring peoples, and the detailed examination of language and customs. Through his writings and teachings he established an 'historical school' of anthropology, marked by *cultural relativism* and detailed studies of individual cultures.

Some European scholars reacted against the work of the evolutionists by arguing that all culture began in one special area, and then spread to other regions. The extreme British *diffusionists*, like Sir Grafton Elliott-Smith and WJ Perry, believed that 'civilization' had originally been invented in Egypt and had then spread, often in diluted or deteriorated form, to other parts of the world!

In 1922, however, three important events occurred which had a profound influence within British anthropology. Rivers, the ethnographer of the Torres Straits Expedition, died. He was the last British field anthropologist to advocate the study of cultures in terms of the diffusion of traits. In the same year, both Bronislaw Malinowski (1884–1942) and Alfred

LEFT *A scene from ancient Egypt, considered by some to be the cradle of civilization. A wall painting showing a celebration with dancing girls and musicians from the tomb of Nebamun at Thebes, 1400 BC.*

ABOVE *A band of musicians on the beach of the Trobriand islands where Malinowski, a 'pioneer of fieldwork' lived and worked.*

RIGHT *All major events from birth to death are marked by special rituals, enabling friends and relatives to express solidarity by gathering together to celebrate or mourn. A buffalo (which will provide food for guests) is sacrificed to honour the lineage gods and the spirit of the dead man at a funeral ceremony in Bulawayo.*

Radcliffe-Brown (1881–1955) published their first extended works of field research. These two figures were to affect British anthropology in ways which are still evident today.

Malinowski was born in Poland, and was educated in maths and natural sciences. Fond of creating myths about himself, he claimed that while recuperating from illness he was converted quite suddenly to anthropology through reading Frazer's *Golden Bough*. Whether this dramatic story about Malinowski is true or not, it is a fact that he came to the London School of Economics in 1910 to study anthropology, and was to spend much of his time until the late 1930s teaching and writing there.

In contrast to the speculative accounts of the 19th century evolutionists, Malinowski asserted the absolute importance of detailed fieldwork, going far beyond the standards established by Boas or Rivers. Indeed, he has been described as 'the pioneer, bush-whacking anthropologist, the originator of the doctrine that until you have lived cheek by jowl with an exotic tribe and spoken their language fluently you cannot claim full professional status' (Lewis, 1976: 54).

Ironically, his most crucial period of fieldwork came about partly by accident. As the First World War broke out, he was in Australia, and as an Austrian citizen was technically regarded as at war with the Commonwealth. Instead of being interned, however, he managed to persuade the Australian authorities to allow him to live and work for two years on the Trobriand Islands, situated to the south-east of New Guinea.

His approach could hardly have been more different from that of Frazer, his supposed inspiration. Although sometimes fond of lurid titles for his works, like *The Sexual Lives of Savages,* he reacted against the idea that these societies were irrational or stupid. Rather than attempt to reconstruct the history of Trobriand peoples, he took an approach which is called *synchronic* – looking at how a society works in the present. He believed that all societies had to solve similar basic problems – how to provide for the physical and psychological needs of

humans. Thus, said Malinowski, every custom or institution, even if it seems strange at first, can be shown to serve a purpose. Marriage can be used to regulate sexual drives, economic institutions attempt to ensure the provision of sustenance, and so on. His approach has come to be called *functionalist*, emphasizing as it does the utility of institutions for serving human requirements.

Like Malinowski, Radcliffe-Brown sought to understand the workings of society in the present, and he produced a related but different form of theory, called *structural-functionalism*. Much of his work was based on the Andaman Islands, situated to the south-west of Burma. Heavily influenced by French sociologists like Emile Durkheim (1858–1917), he avoided what

he saw as Malinowski's over-emphasis on the biological basis of all institutions. He concentrated instead on what he felt was their social functions. Thus, institutions in a given society could be seen as supporting each other, producing stability and solidarity among its members, and maintaining its continued survival.

Particularly in his earlier work, Radcliffe-Brown emphasized the extent to which individuals could maintain 'sentiments' which aided the workings of the group as a whole. One simple illustration of this idea can be seen through his analysis of weeping among the Andaman Islanders. He noted that the shedding of tears, instead of being a spontaneous expression of joy or sorrow, often appeared to be a socially required response to special situations,

ABOVE *These young girls have just been 'married' to the Hindu god Vishnu Narayan in Kathmandu. The belief behind the ritual is that whatever the fate of their mortal husbands, they will never be widowed.*

RIGHT *Before they leave the village for the first stage of their initiation into manhood, boys from the Dinka tribe make a ground nut gruel in preparation for the celebrations marking their return from isolation.*

OPPOSITE, LEFT *The wedding party of a Girahya couple which shows important cultural symbols associated with marriage. The couple are surrounded by female relatives from both families, the bride is covered in her husband's old loin cloth and the groom clutches a sword in his right hand. They are about to 'take rounds of the sacred fire' which will mark the beginning of their new life as husband and wife.*

such as peace-making, marriages or the meeting of long-separated friends. In weeping together, affirming the force of an institutionalized custom, people could be seen as renewing their ties of solidarity. Radcliffe-Brown describes this vividly in the following passage:

> 'On one occasion I asked . . . [them] . . . to show how it was done and two or three of them sat down and were immediately weeping real tears at my request. The weeping in this way is really a ceremony or rite. When two friends or relatives meet who have been separated from one another for a few weeks or longer, they greet each other by sitting down, one on the lap of the other, with their arms around each other's necks . . . .'

In examining the work of Boas, Malinowski and Radcliffe-Brown, we witness the beginnings of the division of interest between some American and British anthropologists. Follow-ing Boas in America, scholars like AL Kroeber (1876–1960) and R Lowie (1883–1957) continued an interest in historical research, as well as a concentration on the analysis of culture. In Britain, the *structural-functionalism* of Radcliffe-Brown was influential until it was criticized for presenting societies as much more stable than they really were. The work of all three men has been superseded by many other approaches to anthropology, and we shall be meeting many of these in later chapters. Nevertheless, Boas, Malinowski and Radcliffe-Brown helped estab-lish some of the features that have continued to characterize the work of anthropologists ever since. They all attempted to develop systematic ways of collecting and analyzing data, and real-ized the importance of explaining particular customs and beliefs in their social and cultural contexts. Malinowski and Boas in particular helped to establish the absolute importance of *fieldwork* for the work of anthropology, and we turn to this in the next chapter.

ABOVE *A Peruvian herdsman in ceremonial dress with whip. He is dressed as a footsoldier to take part in the annual mock battle which brings together men from various villages in the remote highland region of Peru.*

CHAPTER THREE

THE METHODS
OF ANTHROPOLOGY

'MONDAY 1.19.15 . . . Yesterday before noon, Pikana came. With great effort – for he was sleepy, kept yawning, and I had a headache and felt poorly – I wormed out of him material relating to kinship. Then at 12:30 I was so exhausted that I went to bed. After lunch (no appetite), headache. I took injections of arsenic and iron. Began to read Rivers, but had to stop . . . . Around 4 got off my bed with great effort – headache and frightful sluggishness, and went to the village with Igua.'

THE JOYS AND PERILS
OF FIELDWORK

The quotation above is taken from Bronislaw Malinowski's private diary (1967: 66), written while he was working on the Trobriand Islands. The diary was published over twenty years after Malinowski's death, and caused considerable consternation within the anthropological world. The acclaimed hero and exemplary figure of modern practices of fieldwork appeared to be admitting his frailty. Throughout, the diary reveals his constant concern for his health, his sexual frustrations, and frequent irritation with the Trobrianders, his objects of study. The style and content of the diary thus contrast markedly with the confident, seamless prose of the work he produced for public and academic consumption.

In fact, Malinowski was revealing many of the problems and worries of any fieldworker as he or she goes in search of anthropological data. The process of fieldwork is unusual as a technique of research in the sense that it literally takes over the life of the scholar, often for long periods at a time. In order to try to understand how others live and view the world, we cannot simply jet in to their village or town, hire an interpreter and demand to speak to their leader, before hurrying off to another area of study. Rather, the fieldworker must attempt to become immersed in the daily life of those who are studied – whether they are New Guinea tribesmen, American cocktail waitresses or Arctic

OPPOSITE *Mrs Mkize, the Isangoma, a traditional diviner from the Zulu tribe.*

BELOW *It is increasingly common for anthropologists to do fieldwork in their own country. Deborah de Lima (who is Brazilian) takes notes in a village in Amazonia where she spent two and a half years.*

RIGHT *Domestic chores in Ethiopia. A girl pounds maize into paste in the traditional method, adding hot water from a kettle. The Danakil desert, Ethiopia.*

Eskimos. The process of immersion is likely to take at least twelve months, since this is the minimum period required to observe the daily, monthly and yearly rhythms of the social lives of most human communities.

In many academic disciplines, the researcher uses expensive equipment in order to gain information. For the anthropologist, however, the main tools of research are constituted by his or her own ability to form friendships, react sensitively to a variety of puzzling social situations, and perceive patterns in the chaos of everyday life.

The process of carrying out fieldwork has attracted much mystique within the profession. Some scholars would wish to divide the discipline up into those who have passed the test of surviving and even thriving in initially unfamiliar surroundings, and those who have not yet undergone the problems and fascinations of 'culture shock'. The situation is addressed entertainingly and well by the British anthropologist, Nigel Barley, whose initial research did not involve going out 'into the field':

'The profession is full of devoted fieldworkers, skins leathery from exposure to torrid climes, teeth permanently gritted from years of dealing with natives, who have little or nothing of interest to say in an academic discipline. The whole subject of fieldwork, we effete "new anthropologists" with our doctorates based on library research had decided, had been made rather too much of. Of course, older teaching staff who had seen service in the days of empire . . . had a vested interest in maintaining the cult of the god to whom they were high priests. They had damn well suffered the trials and privations of swamp and jungle and no young whippersnapper should take a short cut' (1983: 7).

As Barley suggests, attitudes towards fieldwork are changing. Many scholars now accept that vital historical or analytical work can be carried out in the library. There is no doubt, however, that the practice of fieldwork remains

central to research in social and cultural anthropology, and has formed much of the character of the discipline.

Some reasons can be suggested to account for the mystique attached to this form of research. One relates to the degree of autonomy that it demands. Admittedly, development projects usually involve the cooperation of a number of experts from different fields, concerned with practical problems of aid, agriculture, education, etc. However, purely academic research in anthropology tends to be carried out by a single scholar, working alone.

The period of data collection is extended, often arduous, and frequently involves separation from family and friends at home. Owing to the degree of personal involvement necessary

ABOVE *The experience of contact with another world. A child tries the headphones of a western film crew in Botswana.*

RIGHT *Marriage ceremonies in all cultures contain a rich variety of rituals and customs. This example of some which are familiar to the western eye shows the Tonga Prince Lavaka and his bride cutting the cake on their wedding day.*

for the work, the scholar may develop a firm attachment to what are often (perhaps patronizingly) called 'my people'. In addition, it appears, initially at least, to be very difficult to lay down any specific ground rules which can be said to apply to all kinds of fieldwork. A researcher who journeys to a New Guinea village is likely to be concerned with questions such as the following:

– How can I, a total stranger, become accepted in a society where everybody's social status is dependent upon real or fictitious ties of blood and marriage?

– Will I be able to learn their language, since no dictionary exists?

– What will I find to eat?

On the other hand, the fieldworker who decides to study a local church in the British or American town in which he or she has grown up will not have the same problems of gaining acceptance or subsistence in an initially 'strange' environment. Rather, they are more likely to worry about how they can distance themselves sufficiently from the group in order to provide an academic study of it.

THE POINT OF
THE EXERCISE

Expressed most broadly, the aim of the anthropologist is to provide a description of the social

organization, beliefs and values of a group of people – possibly a village, a church, or a tribe. Thus, the anthropologist acts as a kind of mediator, trying to translate the experience of one way of life into the language and concepts of his or her readers or audience.

In practice, research projects are likely to focus on specific questions, which provide themes for analysis. It is always realized, however, that specific questions about a community can only be answered fully by gaining an *holistic* picture of that community. For instance, an anthropologist may wish to study the relationships between men and women in a village in New Guinea. However, in order to answer such a question a more general picture of life in the village – the economy, ritual practices, types of political authority, etc, must be obtained. Furthermore, factors external to the village might have to be considered, such as the influence of *wage labour* on the migration of men away to distant towns.

Of course, to the extent that we are all interested in social life, in other people, we are all anthropologists. But the process of academic research is much more complicated than a general curiosity about our fellow human-beings. The anthropologist has to try to discover what kinds of behaviour and values are shared within the members of a group or society. This is only possible through painstaking procedures of observation and recording.

ABOVE *Participant observation involves months spent in people's homes, noting the domestic scenes which form a central part of life in the community.*
A Berber woman by the furn (oven) of her hut in Morocco.

43

ABOVE *The homes of new settlers which have been built along the trans-Amazonian highway deep in the Amazonian forests of Brazil.*

METHODS OF INVESTIGATION

For a *natural scientist* such as a chemist, research is often carried out under strictly controlled conditions, in a laboratory specifically designed to aid experimentation. The researcher must know exactly what goes into a test tube, in order to evaluate specific hypotheses and draw conclusions about the reactions of chemicals which are assumed to be uncontaminated by 'foreign' agents.

An anthropologist, however, is a *social scientist,* and this means that the exercise of data-gathering and the formation of conclusions is carried out under radically different circumstances. A fieldworker cannot treat the members of a society as mere objects, to be manipulated according to the whims of research. If anything, he or she is at the mercy of those being studied. The theoretical objective, as in natural science, is not to 'contaminate' or influence the phenomena being studied, but inevitably the very presence of the researcher must make this impossible, since to interact with others – talk to them, eat with them, laugh with them, and so on, is to affect their behaviour.

Fieldwork involves the combining of two apparently very different activities. Participation implies taking part in the everyday life of a community, learning the appropriate language, and, so far as is possible, being taken for granted as a member of the community rather than as a transient tourist. Observation clearly involves a degree of detachment from activities, so that the anthropologist can attempt to see things from a wider perspective. The English anthropologist Stephen Hugh-Jones describes this dual process in discussing his examination of men's rituals among the Barasana Indians of Colombia:

'The first kind . . . [of rite] is held relatively often and I was able to observe a total of nine over a twenty-two month period. At some, I devoted my time to writing notes and making tape-recordings;

at others, I endeavoured to observe them from the inside by dancing with the dancers, playing the . . . instruments, chanting with the chanters and drinking hallucinogenic drugs. The second kind of rite . . . is held very infrequently . . . I was allowed to participate on condition that I did not play the role of the note-taking anthropologist and that I under-went initiation . . . and observed all the relevant prohibitions on diet and beha-viour. My wife remained secluded in the rear of the house together with the other women who assisted her in taking notes' (1979: 16–17).

This passage contains a number of features that tell us about the experience of fieldwork. As a sensitive anthropologist who had gained the trust of the people he was studying, Hugh-Jones was aware of the ambivalent nature of his status among Barasana men. While wishing to observe and analyze their ritual practices from the point of view of an academic, he respected their demand that he take such practices seriously in their own right. Thus, during the second type of ritual he acted entirely as if he were a Barasana man rather than a detached, potentially disturbing presence. Through occasional parti-cipation in rites he could try to understand something of the experience of taking part; through sometimes taking notes and recording rituals, he not only gained a record of what occurred, but experienced the same kind of phenomena from a different, more detached perspective.

In the last part of the extract, he mentions the role of his wife. A common problem for any fieldworker who attempts an holistic study of any community is the part his or her identity plays in controlling the way others react. Some

LEFT A chief and tribal elders in Papua New Guinea.

RIGHT *Women are forbidden to enter the men's hut among the Mehinacu of Brazil where this Shaman is communing with the spirit world by inhaling hallucinogenic smoke.*

of these aspects of identity are of course unalterable. As a male in certain societies, for instance, one may be prevented from having much contact with women – think of the problems of talking to Muslim women in communities where they are kept in isolation by their male relatives. As a young person, one may not gain easy access to older people in communities where relations between the generations are very formal or distant. In the Barasana case,

Hugh-Jones and his wife, also an anthropologist, could of course complement each other's analysis of male-female relations through working as a team, trying to see the ritual from the point of view of both men and women.

The Barasana example illustrates a particular kind of observation, that of specific incidents or situations (in this case rituals) that punctuate ordinary, daily existence. Of course, an anthropologist who wishes to gain a comprehensive picture of the social and cultural life of a community cannot rely on isolated descriptions of unusual or exceptional events alone. Other means of extracting and recording information must be used. The mapping out of the layout of the area of fieldwork, especially if it is a small village, can be a useful way of recording residence patterns and the physical backdrop to all activities. A daily journal is usually written in order to gain a picture of everyday, recurring events as well as deviations from the norm. Personal diaries, such as that written by Malinowski, provide a useful means of recording the state of mind of the fieldworker over a period of time, and how this may affect perceptions of the community being studied.

The object of gathering data is to be able to produce a multi-layered, richly-textured means of describing a society. There is little point in writing journal entries which state: 'Got up, watched a ritual, went to bed', no matter how jaded one is feeling! Pelto, for instance, contrasts what he calls 'vague' and 'concrete' ways of describing an incident:

'*Vague notes*
1. A showed hostility to B.
Concrete notes
2. A scowled and spoke harshly to B, saying a number of negative things, including "Get the hell out of here, Mr B." He then shook his fist in B's face and walked out the room' (1970: 93).

The latter example, although very simple, refers in a short space to:
– the people involved
– the tone of the encounter
– a specific illustration of what was said
– a physical action
– the end of the incident, also indicating its setting.

The kinds of interviews carried out by anthropologists are likely to vary greatly in intention and degree of formality. On one level, the worker may ask questions that appear to arise naturally during a conversation, perhaps while performing other activities with an informant, such as working in a field or sitting in a bar! At the other extreme, and much more formally, the same series of questions may be administered to a selected sample of a given population. In some cases, it may even be appropriate to send out questionnaires in order to elicit responses to questions that usually require factual or yes/no answers.

Some of the dangers of relying naively on information derived from interviews are described by Napoleon Chagnon in his study of the Yanomamō of southern Venezuela. He wished to collect genealogical records from as many people as possible, in other words their statements concerning their relations with others through marriage and common parentage.

RIGHT *Tomb buildings in a Cairo graveyard provide shelter for thousands of migrants and otherwise homeless people. A detailed survey of the residence pattern may reveal many aspects of social organization. In this case, a survey helped identify the period of the move, the location of tomb guardians who control residence rights, and the identity of migrant's contacts from the area of origin.*

However, the Yanomamō have stringent taboos on the use of their names, and reacted to Chagnon's questions by making up answers. He writes:

> 'I assumed, wrongly, that I would get the truth to each question and that I would get the best information by working in public. This set the stage for converting a serious project into a farce. Each informant tried to outdo his peers by inventing a name even more ridiculous than what I had been given earlier . . .' (1968: 11).

The point is not that the Yanomamō are inveterate liars, but that Chagnon had attempted to obtain information in a way that was culturally inappropriate. As he learned more about the Yanomamō, he gave up the direct, public method of collecting genealogies and concentrated instead on other methods, such as talking in private to people whom he knew well and were willing to give him the information he wanted.

A number of techniques can be used to follow the life of an individual member of society, in order to complement the analysis of group or public situations. In societies where the anthropologist's informants are literate, some of them can be asked to keep diaries of their own activities for a week or more. Through following the movements of an individual over a course of time, the researcher can gain an idea of the full range of relationships that make up a person's social network. More broadly, the *life-histories* of individuals can be recorded through interviews or casual conversation over a period of time. These can provide a useful means of obtaining some idea of the values, beliefs and aspirations of members of a particular society. Andrew Strathern describes below the process of recording the life-story of Ongka, a New-Guinea 'Big-Man', or political leader:

> '. . . surrounded by stone axes, clay pots, and wooden tools from Papua New Guinea's past, Ongka began to talk about his birth and about the value of such tools in the times before the first Europeans

arrived in the early 1930s. At the beginning I prompted him with questions and was interested as he described details I had not heard him mention before – his birthplace, the meaning of his name, his mother's death, his first wife. These were all recorded by a small cassette tape-recorder. Soon he got into the swing of things and I left him to it. I would return to the room from time to time to change the cassette over, and would find him fully engrossed, gesturing and smiling into the microphone' (1979: X).

Although obviously willing to talk to as many people as possible, the fieldworker may find that he develops a special relationship with one or more *key informant*. These are often people who are especially eloquent or who come to know the anthropologist particularly well. There are clearly some dangers in this method of gaining information: how can we assess the extent to which such a person's view on society are affected by his or her age, sex, personality, status, etc? However, when complemented by other methods of data collection, this approach can provide very rich and detailed information, gathered over years through a relationship of mutual trust and considerable understanding. The anthropologist Victor Turner, who wrote about the rituals of the Ndembu tribe of Zambia, dedicated one of his books to his 'friend and educator', a man called Muchona.

From the above, it should be clear that fieldwork is most successful when it employs a very wide range of techniques in order to build up a complete picture of a social group or community. Qualitative impressions of events and people are complemented by quantitative data on such details as the age-range, gender-ratio, and size of the population studied. Some kinds of data collection are 'passive', requiring observation of events rather than any direct intervention; others are more 'active', such as the carrying out of interviews or the administration of *projective personality tests,* requiring the informant

ABOVE *Warriors from the Karamojong tribe examine the potential of a Landrover in Uganda.*

to describe how they perceive pictures or shapes shown to them by the fieldworker. Detailed notes are augmented by tape recordings, enabling the precise analysis of language use, and photographs or moving film. Literature, such as books about or by a community or newspapers articles, can be valuable sources of information, especially for anthropologists working in urban and literate contexts.

Overall, the perceptions of the fieldworker should change the longer he or she participates in the life of a community. First impressions of confusion are replaced by a kind of familiarity, as the researcher learns some of the 'rules' of everyday life. Thus, field notes will contain both the initial experience of 'culture shock' and the process of making some sense out of the social environment. As time goes on, the kinds of questions the anthropologist is interested in may well become more complex. A researcher who carried out fieldwork on a church in Scandinavia remarked to one of the authors that he only felt he did his 'real' work in the last six weeks of his stay, after a year of fieldwork. By this he meant not that he had learnt nothing before that period, but that it was not until the last six weeks that he understood enough to know how to pose the right questions.

ABOVE *A superficial glance misinformed by stereotypes of tribal society might expect this picture to show an aggressive war-dance. In fact the Karamojong bridegroom is dancing with close male friends and kin at a pre-wedding ritual of celebration.*

PROBLEMS OF INTERPRETATION AND DESCRIPTION

Anthropologists have increasingly come to realize that it is impossible to be 'objective' observers of society, soaking up 'facts' and then synthesizing these into what Radcliffe-Brown hoped would become a 'natural-science of society'. Even between members of a given group or society, a clear, common view of cultural values or beliefs may not exist. Admittedly, an anthropologist should approach research in a systematic and in some respects 'detached' way. However, he or she always views the world through lenses coloured by personal experiences, cultural values, and states of mind. Some anthropologists, like the American Clifford Geertz, choose to emphasize the effects field-work can have on the researcher him or herself:

> 'An anthropologist's work tends, no matter what its ostensible subject, to be but an expression of his research experience, or, more accurately, of what his research experience has done to him' (1968: vi).

As a result, the scientific ideal of replicating exactly the same results of any piece of research, as one would attempt to repeat a chemical experiment, is unrealistic. An extreme and well-known controversy over this issue involved two distinguished American anthropologists and their work on a village in Mexico, called Tepoztlan. The first study was carried out by Robert Redfield in the 1920s. He found it to be an idyllic place, in which health and happiness abounded amongst its inhabitants. Almost 20 years later, Oscar Lewis went back to the same community. Instead of harmony, he found suspicion and tension. Of course, we can argue that the village itself had changed over time. However, it is more likely in this case that the respective outlooks of the anthropologists had affected the emphases of their work. Redfield tended to see urban life as a source of moral and cultural disintegration, and thus presented

Tepoztlan as an ideal alternative to the horrors of the city. Lewis, on the other hand, perceived the life of peasants as one of poverty and backwardness, and this view came out in his analysis of the village.

Thus, it is perhaps best to see the study of another society as a complex form of interpretation rather than objective observation. This interpretation should be based on an attempt to understand the way informants perceive themselves and the world around them, as well as the ways they use language to classify their environment. However, this is an attempt which cannot ever truly succeed. Luhrmann describes the process in the following way:

'Fieldwork, it is now understood, does not grant a blanket awareness of the hearts and minds of the fieldworker's chosen society, as if he were a woolly sponge. The fieldworker cannot . . . ever really know what occurs in the mind of any one individual. Fieldwork consists, instead, of a series of conversations, as flexible, tendentious, and idiosyncratic as conversations between individuals often are' (1988: 15).

Similarly, the writing of an anthropological text must be a form of compromise. Imagine the problems of trying to describe a piece of music in words. How can we give the impression of all the instruments of the orchestra playing simultaneously, as well as translate the notion of sound into a very different medium, that of writing? In a way, the writer of a piece of ethnography is faced with similar or even more complex problems. Social life and culture consist of forms of behaviour, patterns of belief, complex interactions between friends and enemies, and changes as well as *regularities* over time. Even though fieldwork can take a year or more, this may not be enough to assess the degree of stability or instability of a society.

LEFT *The complex process of interpretation which comes with contact between people of different cultures. Local children view the world through the lens of visiting documentary makers in Kenya.*

Thus on the one hand the anthropologist cannot work like a novelist, inventing situations, or choosing what is and is not relevant according to artistic criteria. On the other hand, however, the process of writing about human society inevitably distorts reality because it is impossible to render the richness and complicated nature of behaviour and belief in words alone. Even films of other societies cannot really give a full idea of the context in which social activity takes place. Nevertheless, there is a sense in which the very distorting quality of anthropological writing can work to its advantage. Because it simplifies reality, and seeks to find patterns and regularities in behaviour and belief, writing about a society can yield insights which pure participation would not reveal. Thus, it provides a way of 'seeing the wood for the trees'. In the next chapter we shall examine some of the ways anthropologists have managed to provide useful analyses.

ETHICS AND IDENTITY

The following is an extract from a leaflet put out by the Association of Social Anthropologists of the Commonwealth:

> 'Ethical dilemmas and the necessity for choice and compromise occur at all stages of research – in the selection of topic, area or population, choice of sponsor and source of funding, in negotiating access, making "research bargains" and conducting fieldwork, and the publication of findings . . .'

One of the most delicate areas of ethics clearly concerns the relationship the anthropologist has with the community being studied. The process of writing about others is itself a form of exploitation in the sense that the researcher is describing the lives of others for personal gain, and this may occur in situations where those described have little idea of what anthropology is. Sometimes, the knowledge gained can be highly sensitive: it may be contrary to the opinions of a host government or perhaps reveal much about individuals who may not wish their opinions or activities to be broadcast or published. Previously, American researchers in South East Asia and Latin America have allowed data they have gathered to be used by their government for political ends. On a smaller scale, one of the authors knows of a case when the dissertation of a university student caused his informants to lose their jobs as cleaners. In responding to his questions, they revealed a certain level of 'time-wasting' during working-hours. When their employer gained access to the dissertation without the permission of the student, the information gathered in good faith was used to justify their removal from their jobs. It can therefore be seen that a major responsibility of the anthropologist must be to make sure that the welfare of informants takes priority over the objectives of academic research. In such situations, the concealing of informants' identities through the use of pseudonyms is a useful device of the ethnographer.

In an attempt to 'pay back' for the knowledge being gained, the researcher is often able to engage in reciprocal relations with informants. This may involve giving food, medicine, money or other kinds of assistance. However, such a strategy can cause as many problems as it appears to solve. While assuaging the guilt feelings of the fieldworker, it can cause rivalries between parties eager to gain his or her favour, and can on some occasions constitute a clear 'interference' in the way of life of the community. Colin Turnbull has described the case of the Ik tribe of Uganda, a population suffering from the depradations of drought and famine. In response to their desperate economic plight, the Ik resorted to leaving old and dying members of the population to die without food, and mocked those who wished to give them aid. Turnbull gives a moving account of his dilemma in this situation: should he have attempted to tend the terminally sick himself, thus preserving their lives for a short period, or should he have respected the survival strategy adopted by the community as a whole? No simple answer can be given to such questions.

One of the most difficult ethical problems of fieldwork can revolve around the identity of the researcher. Usually, in attempting to gain access to a group, the anthropologist attempts to explain his or her identity and intentions. Sometimes, specific 'mediators' can form a bridge between the newly arrived researcher and the members of the group. In approaching the frequently aggressive Yanomamō, for instance, Chagnon was aided by James Barker, the first 'outsider' to establish permanent relations with the tribe.

While the Yanomamō had little idea of the role of an anthropologist, on some occasions potential objects of study are both fully conscious of the aims of social science, and resolutely opposed to them. Sectarian religious groups provide a common example of this position. On these occasions, the researcher has to make a personal decision: should identity and intention be concealed? If so, the researcher not only has to find suitable means of taking notes in private, but must face a further dilemma concerning the publication of material.

Even where permission to carry out research is granted, a fieldworker may find him or herself under unanticipated pressures. Ken Pryce chose to study West Indian lifestyles in a provincial British city. Having therefore joined a local charismatic church, he found himself almost forced into adopting an identity created for him by his informants:

'What I was discovering was that to learn more about the church from the stand-

BELOW The problems of gaining access to women in strictly segregated societies meant that women's lives were largely neglected by early anthropologists. These Bedouin women work together spinning and weaving, in their secluded quarters in the Western Desert, Egypt.

RIGHT *The elaborate styles of hair dressing of Maasai women in the Kenyan Rift valley.*

THE
METHODS OF
ANTHROPOLOGY

point of ordinary members, I needed to be on the inside as a fully fledged believer. I had no choice therefore but to give in one Sunday morning when I and other un-saved persons like myself were called to the altar and asked if we were ready to be baptized . . . ./Baptism did make a differ-ence to my status . . . I was now treated with a new candour. Individual members would now compete to have me in their homes for dinner...' (1979: 285-6).

THE ANTHROPOLOGY OF OURSELVES

One of the benefits of the experience of field-work and the writing of anthropology is that it encourages us to see our own culture not as something 'natural' or inherently 'correct' but as only one among many that have existed in the past and do so in the present. We thus learn to see ourselves in a new light – possibly an uncomfortable one. Consider the following passage, taken from Horace Miner's description of the Nacirema people:

'Nacirema culture is characterized by a highly developed market economy which has evolved in a rich natural habitat. While much of the people's time is devoted to economic pursuits, a large part of the fruits of these labors and a considerable portion of the day are spent in ritual activ-ity. The focus of this activity is the human body, the appearance and health of which loom as a dominant concern in the ethos of the people' (Am. Anth., 58, 1956: 503).

If the customs of the Nacirema sound familiar, it is of course because Miner has simply used the language of anthropology to describe his own culture, that of the United States! The serious point is that the passage illustrates the distancing potential of anthropology: we can use it to look not only at others, but also at ourselves. It is not only 'the natives' in 'exotic' places who have customs which are culturally relative, and need to be explained.

ABOVE *The exotic,
decorative practices of western
culture: a female Punk in
London's Covent Garden.*

CHAPTER FOUR

ANTHROPOLOGY

AT WORK

SOCIAL and cultural anthropologists assume that humankind is united by a common biological heritage. Their job, therefore, is to describe and analyze cultural diversity – the varieties of beliefs, customs and forms of social organization that are evident among contemporary peoples. The great challenge of the discipline is to combine an appreciation of the uniqueness of every culture with an attempt to produce insights that are relevant to humankind in general. We are now going to look at some of the specific fields of inquiry which have interested anthropologists over the decades. These may be summarized very broadly into a set of questions, each one raising an issue of fundamental importance:

1) How do we reproduce ourselves?
2) How do we maintain orderly relations in society?
3) How do we organize the production and distribution of resources?
4) What are our beliefs about the supernatural, or non-material, world?
5) How do we classify and perceive our environment?

KINSHIP AND
SOCIAL RELATIONS

This section will give an impression of some terms and technical principles involved in the study of kinship. Given the enormous variety in the structure and organization of social groups, it is impossible to cover all the ground in a summary of major ideas. However the following overview is intended to provide readers with enough background details to appreciate the central importance of kinship in anthropology.

WHAT IS KINSHIP?

People usually think of kinship in terms of the successive 'blood' relationships which enable people to distinguish relatives (kin) from non-kin. The social arrangements built around kinship have been a dominant theme in anthropology from the 19th century. This was perhaps largely a result of anthropologists studying tribal societies which were based so centrally on kinship and marriage. In analyzing social life, anthropologists had to make sense of kinship to make sense of anything else. Even where people were competing for political power or economic advantage, their actions and decisions were likely to be influenced by ideas of kinship. Malinowski, in his classic study of the Trobriand islanders, described how groups which organized food production and distribution were based on networks of obligation defined by kinship and marriage.

However it is dangerous to assume that kinship is simply a matter of blood relationships. The relationship between the social and the natural world has always intrigued researchers of social life. One area where there is a clear

OPPOSITE *A family from the nomadic pastoralist people of Inner Mongolia where lineage membership is an important feature of social organization.*

RIGHT *A group of brothers pose on their bike in a Dogon village, Mali.*

overlap between nature and society is kinship. This is well illustrated by Rodney Needham's definition of kinship:

> 'The study of kinship is the investigation of how social ties of descent and marriage are established, elaborated, fabricated, modified, forgotten and suppressed; how these ties are related to other manifestations of personal and social action.'

The study of kinship raises a number of questions about how these relationships actually work and how they are perceived by people themselves. For instance, there is the obvious problem of distinguishing 'physical' from 'social' parents.

Following LH Morgan, anthropologists usually refer to the social parents as *pater* and *mater,* as opposed to the physical parents, the *progenitor* and *progenitrix*. The crucial distinction is between the person who is recognized or accepted as a child's father or mother and the person who actually – genetically – is the child's parent. The Lakher of Burma believe that two children with the same mother but different fathers are not relatives at all. Some Australian Aborigines appear to deny men any physical role in reproduction and pregnancy is thought to be brought about by spiritual beings.

In this respect it is safest to broaden the scope of our definition. Roger Keesing defines kinship relationships as 'connections modeled on those conceived to exist between a father and child and between a mother and child' (1976: 217). Although people may conceptualize the biological connection between father and child and mother and child in different ways, it is the social relationship which is most important to anthropologists.

WHAT KINSHIP DOES

Within society kinship is commonly used for two interrelated purposes. First, it is a way of transmitting status and property from one generation to the next, and second, it serves to establish and maintain different categories of social groups. People have to be able to distinguish between kin and non-kin in questions of inheritance. This involves rules and notions of descent which allow specific individuals to be classed as closer relations than others.

TRACING KINSHIP

Networks of kinship ties are created when individuals trace relationships through their parents. These networks are most visible at important events in a person's life such as a wedding, birth or funeral. The group of people that come together in celebration or mourning tends to be dominated by one's kin and in-laws (affines). However a complete kinship network might involve very large numbers and since kinship ties will overlap, smaller and more exclusive groups are needed to form basic social units. This is particularly important in societies which organize their economic or political activity through groups based on kinship.

DESCENT SYSTEMS

Unilineal descent describes the principle which gives a person membership of a kinship group by tracing a relationship through one parent only. One key advantage of unilineal descent is that membership is unambiguous, as are concepts of ownership, rights and duties. For inheritance purposes the closest kin are defined according to rules of descent. This determines who receives property and status.

LEFT *A ritual offering is made to ancestral deities in Dhulikhal, Nepal. The old man is the head of the lineage and acts as a priest, leading the sacrificial ritual.*

CLANS AND LINEAGES

Descent groups may differ in size. A group which includes all the people who consider that they are descended from a common ancestor is called a clan. The ancestor in question may be an historical human being, a mythical figure or a spirit or animal. The usual operational unit of the kinship system is smaller than the clan and is called the lineage. This includes people who can trace actual descent from a known ancestor. *Lineages,* like clans, are *corporate groups* in the sense that they act as a body by owning an area of land or by having legal responsiblity for their members. In all cases the important factor is that the principles for group membership grow from a claim of descent from a common founding ancestor or ancestress.

PATRILINEAL AND MATRILINEAL DESCENT

People can trace descent in two different ways, one is called a *patrilineal* system and the other a *matrilineal* system. Most tribal societies have adopted a *patrilineal* system which recognizes the male line or the father's side as dominant in questions of descent and inheritance. In the less common *matrilineal* systems status and property are transmitted through women. For example, a man's inheritance will go not to his own son, but to his sister's son in such societies. Why inheritance does not solely involve women in matrilineal societies is explained by the obvious fact that authority and property remain mostly in male hands in all cultures.

There are also cases where both lines of descent are used for the purposes of inheritance, each in a different context. The Yako of Nigeria attach equal importance to both matrilineal and patrilineal lines of descent: a man's property, land rights and ancestral spirits pass through the male line, and moveable property like livestock, currency and household goods pass in the maternal line. However even where one line of descent is given great emphasis, some significance is almost always attached to what John Beattie calls the 'submerged' line. In many patrilineal societies witchcraft or supernatural powers are considered to pass through the female line. Conversely, among the strongly matrilineal Ashanti of Ghana a spiritual element called *ntoto* is inherited patrilineally.

DESCENT, ANCESTORS AND LAND

It is important to note that descent is a process across time. Descent systems are a means of defining continuity with the past, or specifying relations among the living through the ties they have with long-dead ancestors. Some peoples, such as Australian Aborigines, define their relationship to territories in terms of spiritual connections through ancestors.

FICTIVE KINSHIP

Anthropologists have recognized that descent only entitles a person to be a member of an actual group, whether partilineal or matrilineal. Whether they are members or not depends on ordinary facts of life like individual circumstances and choice. When people claim relationships to others who do not fulfill the requirements of actual kinship, this is called *fictive kinship*. However, these relationships often have the same emotional and obligatory force as those between blood relatives. One simple way of thinking about this comes from our own notions of foster parents or the way a child might call a close family friend who is not an actual relative 'auntie' or 'uncle'.

THE FAMILY UNIT

In all societies there is some form of what can be called a family group, recognised as a discrete and bounded social entity. What may differ is the composition of the group, the social importance attached to different members and relationships, and the underlying *social norms* and values governing local perceptions of kinship. Robin Fox has argued that anthropologists should consider the family less as an institution or unit and more as a 'field of action'. Within this 'field' various bonds operate for various purposes and 'it is the purposes which influence which bonds will be forged, which strengthened, which ignored' (1975:74). Fox's anthropological interest centres on explanations for forms of family arrangements. He argues that the basic social unit is that of mother and child and the basic problem in human and social terms is provisioning and protecting this unit. The

BELOW A blacksmith making spears and hoes for the Dinka tribe. Although he lives and works among the Dinka he is not from the same tribe, but an adopted member of the community.

nuclear family of mother, father and children is, in Fox's view, just one of the more common solutions to this problem.

The general point is that factors such as marriage, domestic arrangements, sexual access and legal authority must be seen as independent variables. An example of an alternative arrangement will demonstrate the differences that can exist in family organization, and also how the 'independent variables' of marriage or sex might influence the form and content of family life. Among the Nayar of Malabar, men (as the fathers of children), have no legal or domestic status *vis-a-vis* their wife's household. The bond that is activated for the care and protection of mother and child is that of brother and sister. When a woman marries and has children, the children must return to the mother's family on puberty, making the nuclear family of man-woman-child only one phase of a continuing domestic cycle.

ABOVE *Three generations of an extended family from Inner Mongolia inside the ger (portable tent) which they share as a largely self-sufficient domestic unit.*

LEFT *An all-female ritual among Amazonian Indians. The women are celebrating the power and bravery of a warrior ancestress who cut off one breast in order to make her arrows more swift before a crucial battle.*

RIGHT *A newly-wed couple from the Karamojong outside the marital hut where they will live as a domestic unit separate from both sets of kin.*

MARRIAGE RULES

The descent group also plays a prominent role in regulating marriages in society. This often takes the form of rules which forbid members of the same lineage or clan to marry each other. If people are required to marry outside the lineage or clan they belong to, this is called a rule of *exogamy* (out-marriage). The opposite rule of *endogamy* is where people must marry within a defined group or community. Patrilineages are usually *exogamous;* members being prohibited from marrying each other. Some anthropologists have considered this to be an 'extension' of the prohibition against incest, which exists in some form in all societies. Robin Fox has described *exogamy* as 'the familial incest taboo writ large'.

THE PURPOSE OF MARRIAGE

Marriage has been defined generally as 'a union between a man and a woman such that children born to the woman are considered to be the legitimate offspring of both parents'. The main point is that marriage creates new social relationships, rights and duties between the spouses and their kin, and establishes the rights and status of children when they are born.

With regard to different types of marriage, a society's rules may require *monogamy* – that each spouse have a single partner, or permit *polygamy* – that one or other spouse may be simultaneously married to other partners. The commonest form of polygamy is the marriage of one man to several wives (*polygyny*), but *polyandry* (the marriage of a woman to a number of men) exists in only a few societies. The rights transferred in marriage as well as the type of marriage is closely related to rules of descent and inheritance. For instance the rights a husband acquires differ markedly between *patrilineal* and *matrilineal* societies. The quantity of money, goods and valuables which are exchanged when a marriage takes place also differ in this respect.

MARRIAGE PAYMENTS

Anthropologists often focus on marriage as a contractual agreement between different parties, examining the rights and valuables tranferred, and the various economic and political interests served by the contract. *Bridewealth* and *dowry* are the two main types of payments which accompany marriage. Both are related to notions of descent and the rights which are transferred between the parties involved.

Bridewealth most often occurs in patrilineal descent systems where the bride's family have given a man the means of continuing his name and line, and expanding his household. The bridewealth a man or his family pays may be taken as a public sign of the importance of the marriage and the rights he has acquired in the woman and her children. In simple terms dowry may be interpreted as a 'payoff' to the woman who is marrying out of her own family. It represents her share of the family estate.

If we examine one study of dowry we can see how marriage payments have both a practical

ABOVE *A Japanese bride in the traditional highly-coloured marriage kimono at a wedding in Tokyo. In contrast to the bride, her attendants are dressed in ceremonial black costumes.*

LEFT *The conspicuous display of gifts of money and valuables is associated with marriage in many cultures. Guests at a Sikh wedding in London congratulate the newly-wed couple, and shower them with coins and bank notes.*

and a symbolic importance. DB Rheubottom argued that *dowry* in Yugoslav Macedonian society focusses attention on the bride's past and future social roles. These roles are reflected in the different gifts given. For example household goods, particularly kitchen utensils, represent the bride's role as a wife. Furniture, foodstuffs and bed linen are given which emphasize the bride's future roles in reproduction, motherhood and nurturing. These gifts also mark the end of a woman's dependence on her own family and her place within her new husband's home.

It is also important to consider *dowry* and *bridewealth* in terms of the new social relationships established by marriage. The gifts and valuables given on marriage demonstrate the givers' faith in the marriage and the importance of the new bond linking families. The higher the investment, the better the couple's economic foundation for married life. Since there is usually an

agreement that gifts will be returned on divorce, the greater the investment made, the more efforts will be made to keep a marriage intact. However in his study of Bedouin *bridewealth*, E Peters argues that we should not overstress the economic side of marriage. In this society, the intervention of concerned family members and friends has as much impact on the marital relations as the size or complexity of any traditions of dowry or bridewealth:

> 'Material goods do not hold human beings together . . . marital stability is rooted in the moral context created by a community, symbolically expressed by the animals (or goods) which change hands at several stages on the way to a union' (1980:151).

It is useful to end this discussion of marriage rules and practices with an example of a very unusual type of marriage: the 'ghost marriage'

RIGHT *A formal wedding pose of bride and groom with their attendants at the couple's new home on Baffin Island.*

of the Nuer of the Sudan described by Evans-Pritchard. In a striking way it shows how key concepts in the field of kinship like lineality, descent and cultural notions of parenthood are inextricably linked.

The Nuer consider that every man has the social right and duty to marry and produce offspring. If a man dies before he can marry, or a father has no sons, then it is his closest kinsman's duty to pay the necessary bridewealth and 'marry a wife in his name'. The children of this marriage are taken as the dead man's children. It is also possible for a Nuer woman to provide the cattle required for bridewealth and so establish the right to count another woman's children as her own. The 'woman-husband' as she is known nominates a man to cohabit with her 'wife' (the woman paid for with the bridewealth) and she has the same rights as a husband – even being able to claim compensation if the woman commits adultery.

This section has given an overview of some of the terms and concepts involved in the study of kinship. Anthropologists have found that whether the direct focus of study is descent groups or marriage payments, cultural ideas about kinship and affinity involve a myriad of other elements of the social world. These kinship terms will crop up throughout the following sections and show how a society's view of kinship and descent influence peoples' political, legal and economic activity.

'WARRE' AND ORDER: THE ANTHROPOLOGY OF POLITICS AND LAW

Writing in the 17th century, Thomas Hobbes asserted that humankind is presented with a stark choice: either we can live in a state of anarchy ('warre'), or we can accept the need for civil obedience. In a state of 'nature', according to Hobbes, humans are free of constraints but also aggressive and rapacious. Thus civilization can only come with the rule of the state and the sovereign.

ABOVE *A Baladi ('belly')
dancer employed to entertain
the male guests at a wedding
feast in Cairo. In poor
Muslim districts, male and
female guests have separate
celebrations. Women stay
indoors chatting and story-
telling. The men's
celebrations are more
unrestrained.*

RIGHT *A wrestling match among Amazonian Indians. In former times the purpose of the match was to decide the leader of a raiding party before it set off to capture another tribe's weapons and women.*

For the majority of readers of this book, who live in western, industrialized societies, it would appear as though the choice has been made. We no longer have all-powerful sovereigns, but we inhabit nation-states in which the maintenance of law and order and the practice of politics have become specialized and well-organized enterprises. Judges and lawyers go through years of training before they can understand legal systems which appear baffling to the lay person. Politicians seek to gain popular support for the right to control public policy and resources. Police forces and armies, subject to the state, are instructed to use necessary force to maintain internal order or external boundaries.

In many of the small-scale, 'face-to-face' communities studied by anthropologists, however, the situation is very different. The careful distinctions that we try to make between our economic, legal and political systems are not necessarily evident. The centralized rule of a sovereign or a state administration may be absent or remote. Indeed, to use words like 'judge', 'law' or 'court' in such circumstances may be hopelessly inappropriate.

Nevertheless, it is clear that, contrary to Hobbes' belief, such communities have not descended into chaos or anarchy. The question we need to ask, therefore, is how are regular social and political relations maintained? Some 19th century writers had firm ideas about the development of order in human history. The evolutionist Sir Henry Maine argued that societies could be seen as progressing from an emphasis on 'status' to one based on 'contract'. In other words, earlier societies defined the rights and obligations of a person according to his or her fixed position in, for instance, a descent group. As society developed, however, people could be seen to act more autonomously, entering as individuals into new relationships for specific aims and purposes.

Emile Durkheim, the French sociologist, chose to contrast societies bound by *mechanical solidarity* with those characterized by *organic solidarity*. In the former, the social group is held together since people largely share skills, cus-toms, and beliefs. In the latter type of society (like our own), people live in a whole range of very different ways, performing specialized jobs which complement and therefore rely on each other. Cooperation depends on the fact that no single person can perform all the necessary tasks of existence for him or herself.

Although both Maine and Durkheim made useful analytical points, they overemphasized the extent to which people in so-called 'primitive' societies were constrained by fixed statuses or common beliefs, rather than acting in innovative and idiosyncratic ways. Nowadays, we realize that we cannot see any community or society as working like a well-oiled machine, with each component combining perfectly to produce standardized and repeated results *ad infinitum*.

On the one hand, we are all strongly influenced by cultural conventions. The 'rules' of society must be sufficiently comprehended and obeyed for a minimum amount of cooperation, predictability of behaviour and mutual understanding. As Keesing states:

'The man who robs a bank is, in sociological terms, criminally deviant. But the anthropologist can perceive him as a routine-bound conformist as well. He

BELOW *The labour of the family group is required to construct the ger or yurt, the transportable dwelling of nomads in Inner Mongolia.*

RIGHT *All societies have norms defining appropriate male and female activities. A grandmother washes dishes, helped by her grandson in a Cairo slum. This 'unmasculine' behaviour will be unthinkable when the boy is a few years older.*

comes to the bank appropriately clothed, walking rather than crawling, on the sidewalk rather than the roof or the gutter. He utters or writes his demands in hopelessly conventional English, and he makes his getaway on the right side of the street . . . . A Trobriand islander would be hard-pressed to rob an American bank' (1981: 317).

On the other hand, it can be argued that individuals everywhere are engaged in 'transactions' with each other, manipulating language, re-interpreting social norms and altering appearances for personal ends.

In a sense, all social groups have similar basic problems to solve. As the British anthropologists Fortes and Evans-Pritchard pointed out (1940), not all societies have 'government' in the sense of an administration with specialized personnel. However, we can say that some kind of political organization is present in all societies. In other words, people everywhere must devise ways to control resources within given areas or territories, settle disputes, or perhaps act together in the face of external threats. Not every society has laws in the sense of precedents or rules recorded in specialized language, but all do have *norms* (explicit or implicit) which people are supposed to respect, and *sanctions* to punish those who offend the standards of public opinion.

Anthropologists have usually divided up the range of human societies into a number of very broad categories, based on their forms of political and economic organization:

HUNTERS AND GATHERERS

Some peoples live by hunting animals and gathering food which grows naturally in the environment, rather than cultivating crops or raising livestock. Examples include Eskimos, Australian Aborigines or the case we shall consider here, the !Kung of the Kalahari Desert of southern Africa.

The way of life of many of the !Kung depends on their being mobile. Small bands of 20 to 60 individuals move throughout the landscape. Each is made up of a handful of families, and a man may have two or more wives. Every band has a territory, which means that its members have the right to gather food from that territory and use its waterholes. Membership of a band is reasonably flexible, depending partly on marriage but also on personal choice and the availability of resources.

The environment, combined with the !Kung's strategy for survival, require them to live at a low population density. Furthermore, material resources are not valued, not least because they would simply be a burden to a mobile lifestyle. The ability to survive depends more on knowledge and individual skill than the use of complex technology. The !Kung thus pursue what Sahlins (1972) has memorably called 'the Zen road to affluence'. Instead of measuring status in terms of the acquisition of more and more wealth and possessions, as in our consumer society, they carry out a way of life which satisfies material desires that are kept to the minimum.

For the !Kung, the political and economic institutions that we have developed are therefore irrelevant. They do not need to coordinate large numbers of people in long-term and unified associations, or control the use of large amounts of stored resources. Although cooperation is useful, and food such as meat is often shared, families and individuals are reasonably self-reliant. Each band has a headman who is chosen by consensus, but he has little power other than some influence over the group's movements. His position is likely to depend on his ability to organize and maintain good relations among band members.

TRIBAL SOCIETIES

Like hunters and gatherers, members of tribes do not depend on central organizations to maintain political or economic relations. However, they tend to bring together larger groups of people, who often share a common language and culture. They usually derive food from cultivation of foodstuffs and/or the herding of animals.

Tribes can be organized in a number of ways. Voluntary associations, like secret societies, can bring people together. Village councils can make important decisions on public matters. Very often, people maintain rights and duties

ABOVE *Women are often expected to perform the bulk of labour-intensive work in small-scale agricultural societies. This woman, chewing a reed for moisture, returns laden with water pots from the well in Dupte, Ethiopia.*

towards each other through monitoring their mutual relations of kinship or descent. Thus, political organization may centre around the clan, an association of people who regard themselves as having descended from a common ancestor, even though their exact genealogical links may be unclear.

One important way of determining the rights and duties of members of a given society, apart from dividing male from female roles, is to distinguish between people according to their age. In our society, after all, we talk of 'school children', 'mature adults' 'pensioners', and so on. Through *age-set* systems, people are united in ways which cross–cut the bonds of kinship. Young people are grouped together in a named unit, which stays together as its members grow older and new sets are formed from later generations. Younger sets treat older ones with respect, and perhaps perform services for them. Members need not live together, but this can occur. Among the Zulu of southern Africa,

ABOVE *Dinka boys in the 'fattening camp' where they live in isolation from the rest of the community as a trial which leads to their initiation into manhood.*

young men were treated as warriors, cut off from the normal ties of the community. Perhaps a weak parallel can be found in our society by looking at generations of school or university students, who often grow up together and maintain contact throughout the whole of their lives.

A classic study of tribal organization was carried out by Evans-Pritchard (1940). He examined the Nuer of the swamps and savannahs of the Sudan, and described them as existing in a form of 'ordered anarchy'. Over 200,000 people shared a common culture, language, and economy, as they cultivated crops in villages or dispersed to cattle camps according to the season. They were split into tribes numbering between five and 45,000 people.

The Nuer had no chiefs or strong political leaders. However, political and clan organization combined in a fascinating way. The largest territorial and political group was the 'tribe', which was then divided into smaller and smaller 'neighbourhoods' or 'districts' until the smallest political unit, the village, was reached. As the levels of segmentation got smaller and smaller, so the groupings became more and more cohesive. Each tribe was also associated with a dominant clan, which could in turn be divided into smaller and smaller units, corresponding to the hierarchy of political groupings. The smaller the unit, the closer people were united by genealogical links derived from the dominant clan. Disputes often occurred within a tribe – over cattle, property, or adultery – but the level of violence expected between disputants would vary according to their closeness in genealogical and political terms. Within a village, people would fight with wooden clubs only, while between distant villages violent and protracted feuds could develop. As Kuper puts it:

'If a man in one village killed a man in another, the two villages would mobilize to settle the debt. If a man in one of these villages killed a man in another district, the two villages would unite with other villages in their district against the villages of the other district' (1973:114).

LEFT *The much revered
Lamas from the Tamang
ethnic group, who live in the
hills north of Kathmandu, are
welcomed on their arrival in
the city for a temple festival.*

ABOVE *Healers and those in
contact with the supernatural
or spirit world are highly
respected and often feared.
Their often nomadic lifestyle
reinforces their status as one
outside and beyond the
community.*

This principle of 'segmentary opposition' is perhaps best rendered by the Arab proverb: 'I against my brother; my brother and I against my cousin; my cousin, my brother and I against all outsiders'. Ultimately, a Nuer tribe could combine together in opposition to the largest possible equal and opposite unit – another tribe.

Many have criticized aspects of Evans-Pritchard's analysis. However, his work was important in revealing how a degree of social organization could occur through series of temporary alliances, that ultimately could embrace very large amounts of people. He also illustrated the dual nature of conflict: in one sense it is destructive, in that it brings violence and conflict; however, it can also have an integrative function, bringing people together who would otherwise remain apart. Think, for instance, of a modern nation preparing for war against a foreign power: differences of creed and class are often forgotten temporarily in the face of a common threat.

CHIEFDOMS

Chiefdoms necessarily involve ranking of people as well as centralized authority. Individual status may be determined by position in a *descent group*. The chief, often the inheritor of the office, serves to unite a series of levels of administration, and may take on a number of functions, as the re-distributor of resources, ultimate judge, and religious functionary.

Keesing has summarized the case of the Polynesians of the Hawaiian Islands (1981: 291-2). He describes how society was based on three hereditary social classes – commoners (the most numerous), nobles and inferiors. Commoners supplied nobles with tribute, and regarded them as sacred. It was believed that the ranking of nobles was based on descent from the gods.

Islands were divided into chiefdoms, each ruled by a 'paramount chief' who was seen as having absolute powers conveyed to him by his high god. His authority was consolidated and put into practice by priests, counsellors, military leaders, and local, lesser chiefs. Thus the paramount chief combined secular powers and religious authority. His connection with the divine order implied that he was more than a mere mortal, and therefore in theory could not be questioned. Such a claim contrasted with his actually rather unstable position. In practice, he needed to validate his authority through being victorious in battle, and *succession* was subject to much intrigue.

The Polynesian case illustrates an important aspect of political relations, particularly in hierarchical societies: the exercise of authority. In order to control the lives of others, individuals such as chiefs must prove their status is beyond the common run of humans. In Polynesia, we saw how a chief's actually rather precarious position was partly concealed by his association with a divine and unchanging order. For a Marxist, such a disguising of political and economic realities with a religious veil could be called a form of 'mystification.' This does not mean to say that chiefs consciously and cynically manipulated their position through deceiving their naive subjects: they were as likely to believe in their divinely inspired superiority as anybody else.

THE STATE

Here, the individual is treated as a citizen of a territorially-defined political unit. Thus the status derived from birth in a particular descent group becomes less important than it is in a chiefdom. State organization involves the complex coordination of social and economic classes such as slaves, merchants, bureaucrats, priests and politicians. The invention of literacy, allowing the easy accumulation, transport and storage of information, has proved invaluable to the development of many states.

The kinds of societies we have described above should not be seen as isolated from each other or as unchanging entities. The categories mentioned are crude approximations of a reality that is very complicated. Many hunter-gatherers, including the !Kung, have connections with societies very different from their own. Some anthropologists have argued that the idea of the tribe as a cohesive political unit comes largely from colonial administrators, anxious to define and therefore control the organization of 'native' peoples. Nor should the categories be ranked in an evolutionary schema: everyday life in a hunter-gatherer society is not necessarily 'simpler' than life in a western state in any but a technological sense.

However, chiefdom and state societies do differ from hunter-gatherer and tribal societies over the degree of centralized control of people and resources. The latter is achieved through the appropriation of authority, material goods and the use of force by specialized and élite groups.

BELOW *A chief in Western Samoa displaying the elaborate costume which distinguishes him from commoners and indicates his wealth and status.*

ABOVE *Nomads from a number of different groups meet at a market to trade and restock their supplies in Rajasthan, India.*

This contrast can be brought out further by looking briefly at a subject that has been of importance to anthropology: *dispute settlement*. All societies need ways of regulating conflicts between members. These may arise over competition for resources, or disagreements over the 'rules' of social life. Durkheim believed that 'simpler' societies would resolve conflicts by clearly identifying and suppressing deviations from shared social norms. However, anthropological study has revealed the large range of ways in which *norms* in any society can be interpreted, especially where no written records exist.

Many methods exist for controlling the actions of others, even before they have committed any 'wrong'. As we are all aware, even

such an apparently trivial action as gossip can, in the right circumstances, be an effective form of social control.

In those cases where specific conflict arises, action may be channelled into controlled ritual rather than potentially destructive violence. One strategy used in Eskimo groups is the *song-duel*. Here, two parties confront each other before the assembled community, and pour abuse over each other in the form of improvised songs. The winner emerges through public acclaim. Thus a resolution is found that is sanctioned by the community, grievances are aired, and even a degree of entertainment provided.

Accusations of witchcraft, or at least the threat of them, are also effective in some communities. The witch is perceived to be the opposite of all that is good, and thus the fear of being called a witch and dealt with accordingly can encourage conformity to norms. Evans-Pritchard showed that among the Azande of the Sudan an individual that was regarded as too aggressively successful could be accused of harming others through witchcraft. Some anthropologists have seen McCarthyism in the USA of the 1950s as a form of witch-hunt that got out of hand. Senator McCarthy regarded Communism as an absolute evil, and was able to allege with little or no justification that many Americans were tainted by being associated with this political creed.

In all societies, mediators can play useful roles in ensuring that conflict does not escalate into damaging violence. Although they may lack formal powers of coercion or the law, they can act as 'neutral' bridges between people who are estranged. Leopard-skin chiefs among the Nuer are 'earth-priests' who are believed, in some anthropological accounts at least, to have no real political power. The perpetrator of a murder or injury can seek asylum with the 'chief', who can then attempt to negotiate the payment of compensation to the aggrieved party in order to avoid the escalation of a violent feud.

The methods of solving disputes may be related to the kinds of social relations normal to a community. In the West, we have become used to what are sometimes called 'single-purpose relations' with others: our employer is not usually our parent or our priest as well. However, in many communities arranged on a smaller and more 'intense' scale, people may relate to each other through several different roles. Like the different threads that combine to make a section of rope or string, these relationships are 'multi-stranded', involving perhaps economic, religious and kinship obligations. Consequently, conflicts between individuals may cause serious disruption in the course of everyday life. As scholars like Victor Turner showed, any given dispute may act to dramatize and rekindle many earlier, latent conflicts.

Thus methods of resolving disputes may be more concerned with making sure that people are willing to carry on cooperating with each other than with producing a black-and-white decision, and perhaps causing enmities that cannot be healed. Among the Kpelle of Liberia, for instance, people can avoid using formal courts by holding *moots*. In these, kin and neighbours can get together to resolve domestic problems and, under the auspices of a mutually respected mediator, negotiate a solution. This method gives them a flexibility that is difficult to achieve in the formal surroundings of a typical court-room (though the latter was often imposed by colonial administrators). In formal courts, trained specialists who have no connection with the disputants are obliged to apply written, legal precepts that apply to everybody equally. It thus becomes difficult to take into

BELOW *A diviner of the Azande tribe with the rodent's skull he uses to make predictions and work spells.*

ABOVE *Old men greet each
other at an Oboo ceremony in
Ordos, Inner Mongolia. A
ritual specialist has set out
incense and ritual equipment
on a small mobile altar near
the mausoleum of Ghengis
Khan, the greatest hero of the
Mongol nation.*

account the unique nature of every case. Consider the following passage, describing an English court of law:

> 'Black robes and white wigs mark out the legal specialists – lawyers, judges and clerks. They also depersonalize the individuals and have connotations of sobriety, age (and by association wisdom) and tradition. The costume adds authority especially to the judge who is only seen in this garb . . . . Courtroom ritual has the effect of enhancing the sanctity, inaccessibility and impartiality of the law, represented in the person of the judge. It cannot be approached directly by individuals but only through specialist intermediaries, the lawyers' (Yong, 1985: 79).

We might admire the impartial administration of justice that such a court seeks to maintain. However, we must accept that it also contains much that is less comforting, and which contrasts with the flexibility and sociability of a moot. The price of impartiality is the impersonality that characterizes much of life in a western society.

ANTHROPOLOGY AND ECONOMIC ACTIVITY

A Solomon islander inspects his most valuable possessions, a bag of shells strung together. He has five shells, but must have at least seven before he can present them at the next feast honouring his ancestors. If he could get three or four more shells, people would consider him to be a very important local figure and the feast would be a huge success. He is also worried about his gardens. He could sacrifice a pig to the ancestor who is causing the poor yield, but to pay for a pig he would have to break up his shell collection. Alternatively he might get the pig he needs for the sacrifice by teaching a neighbour some curing magic. The biggest problem of all is how to contribute to the cost of his cousin's marriage without using one of the most precious shells. If he makes a miserly contribution then this man's powerful father will refuse to contribute to the forthcoming feast, and that would mean a considerable loss of face in the community.

ECONOMIC DILEMMAS?

The alternatives being considered by the islander involve how to make the best use of available resources. In the terms of an economist, he is seeking to maximize goals by allocating resources strategically. The resources at the Solomon islander's command include his magical knowledge, his pigs, crops and the highly valuable shell collection. In addition, there are the favours owed to him and his labour (which he cannot exchange for shell valuables). The most important objective is to acquire more shells. However, importantly, the shells will not bring any material advantage. From the islander's point of view what is most valuable is the prestige he will get by giving the shells away.

LEFT *The sifting of manioc grains in rural Amazonia. This is the final stage of the long process of making manioc flour. After the manioc roots are harvested they are soaked in water, when soft they are peeled, grated and squeezed to remove the poisonous juices. The grains are roasted and then sifted before grinding into flour for local use or trade.*

BELOW LEFT *Fishing in Sri Lanka. The time, effort and outcome of different methods of producing food are a key element in many studies of economic activity in small-scale societies.*

RIGHT *Cheese production in
the Danakil desert of
Ethiopia. The young girl tests
the goat's milk as she shakes it
in the 'churning pouch'.*

THE ANTHROPOLOGIST AS ECONOMIST?

Can the basic assumptions of western economics explain the islander's behaviour? Should anthropologists consider magic or shells as resources to be allocated among alternative goals (like keeping the ancestors happy)? Can we apply our own notions of scarcity or profit-making to analyses of non-western societies where 'economic activity' has no obvious monetary or material value? The debate is not so much that other societies have a different type of economic organisation, (this is quite evident), but whether it is a difference of *kind* or *degree*. If it is a difference of degree, then there are concepts from western economics which can be useful. If it is a difference of kind, then anthropologists need to develop their own concepts to understand economic activity in other cultures.

FORMALISM AND SUBSTANTIVISM

Such questions underpinned a debate among anthropologists about the use of western economic theory. The two positions referred to above became known as Formalism and Substantivism. The Formalists argued that western economic theory could be applied to the study of non-western economies. Lionel Robbins' classic view of economics as 'relationships between ends and scarce means which have alternative uses' (1925:16) indicated a type of behaviour which could be found in all societies. In simple terms economic decision-making concerned the use of limited resources such as land and labour. The Substantivists argued that a new definition of economic activity was needed, one which could make sense of societies without easily identifiable kinds of markets or money.

The crux of the problem lay in the fact that economic activity in non-western societies appeared too closely tied up with other forms of behaviour. As in the case of the Solomon islander, it was too difficult to identify a distinct economic sphere. In other words, anthropologists must view the economic and the social as bound together, since economic activity is clearly constrained by human activity.

LEFT *The busy market which serves local traders and nomadic peoples from distant areas in Mysore, India.*

RIGHT *Dinka men and boys work together to carve a 'dug out' canoe from a tree trunk.*

A DIFFERENCE OF DEGREE

A Formalist might argue that the differences between western and non-western economies are only superficial. People everywhere make rational choices about the use of their resources. In short the difference between primitive and western economies is only one of degree.

A DIFFERENCE OF KIND

Karl Polanyi, an economic historian, and his disciple George Dalton, argued that the differences between western and 'primitive' economies were more fundamental. Typical of the Substantivists, they thought that the distinctive features of primitive economies were obscured when its processes were translated into the functional equivalents of western economic life. Certain aspects of primitive economic activities might appear similar to those familiar to western eyes, but this was not to say that they were organized or operated on the same principles. The main point is that questions about a society's economic systems could only be asked and answered in terms of its own values.

SYSTEMS OF PRODUCTION

One central feature of the organization of any society is the division of labour. Every society, assigns different tasks to men, women, the old and the young. Where a society depends on hunting and gathering food, people of the same household are likely to perform many of the tasks necessary for their basic needs, or subsistence, independently. Some *subsistence* activities such as hunting large animals or netting fish require larger groups to work together. It might also be necessary to call on 'specialists' for some part of the task: a priest may bless a new fishing boat or cast a spell to ensure a successful hunt.

The division of labour is sometimes simple enough to ensure that all basic goods can be produced by the people who consume them. At the other extreme, where the division of labour is at its most specialized (as in in a modern city) few people can produce any of the goods they consume themselves. A New Yorker may make a specialized contribution to economic life as a factory worker, and with the wage she receives she can make use of other people's services, and buy the goods she needs through the medium of money.

The organization of productive activities is closely tied to the structure of social groups. All this means is that where hunting or fishing is the main way of providing food, members of the same family, or people who belong to the same household, tend to work together to produce the goods they need. Yet there may also be other informally organized groups of relatives and friends who come together to form *units of production*. Two examples of anthropological studies of production illustrate how closely economic activity is related to the way people live, the values they have and how they perceive the world around them.

THE PRODUCTION OF PRESTIGE

A classic study of social and economic life is Malinowski's *Argonauts of the Western Pacific* (1922), one of his studies of the Trobriand islanders. Trobriand villages are scattered along shallow lagoons on the west coast of the flat coral island and in the interior. No one village has access to all the material goods residents need, and there are some goods which cannot be found anywhere on the main island.

The most important type of production in the island is agriculture. The major crop is the yam. When an area is chosen for cultivation all members of a village form the gardening team which does the work. The garden area is subdivided into squares and each man has several squares which his own household cultivates. Tasks which need the cooperation of a larger group of workers are done by the whole

RIGHT *These sisters are highly skilled weavers who make a large proportion of rugs sold in their father's shop in the Egyptian Delta. They have been weaving since they were about 8 years old and left school to work for the family. They receive no wage for their weaving, which is expected of them as female members of the family and as compensation for the dowries that will have to be paid when they marry.*

gardening team, while everyday daily tasks are the responsibility of each family. All adults play a full part in agricultural production and (apart from the special services of the garden magician) the division of labour is mainly by sex and age. Men cut the scrub, men and women clear the ground for planting, men plant, women weed, and both sexes take part in the harvest. Garden production is one of the most important aspects of life for the Trobriand islanders.

Two factors of production in yam cultivation are crucial. First, the quantity. Everyone aims to produce vast piles of yams, far beyond what a household can eat and people work far harder than is necessary to produce enough to satisfy their food needs. Second, about three quarters of the yams produced are given away. Yams are given in tribute to the chief of a village, to the husband's sister, and to other female relatives in this matrilineal society. People must always give the best and biggest yams they grow, and the better the yams, the greater one's prestige. There are contests of 'gift giving' that are duels for prestige between families and villages. The symbolic rather than material side of yam production is most clearly illustrated by the conspicuous display of highly valued yams which are never eaten. These yams, left to rot in storehouses, especially by villagers of high rank, become symbols of the owners' power and importance.

THE DOMESTIC MODE OF PRODUCTION

The *domestic mode of production* is a term which refers to a productive system of small-scale societies. In short the domestic 'mode' occurs where production is organized, controlled and carried out by individual household units. Each domestic production unit has all the appropriate tools and resources to provide for the group's subsistence needs.

The domestic mode is a way of producing food for consumption and there is no compulsion to provide a surplus or to exchange what is produced with an eye to a profit. In simple terms productive work stops once people have secured their immediate food requirements. For

example the !Kung only pick enough mangetti nuts (their most important food) to satisfy their food needs. There is no desire to gather those which rot on the ground and sell them. The idea, if it exists, is not acted on.

Culturally-determined levels of 'affluence' operate within, and influence the system of production. In the domestic 'mode' of the so-called primitive economies, (which Sahlins has described as 'the original affluent society'), production is for 'use' rather than profit. Social and cultural values also have their influence on production patterns.

One striking example comes from the Lele and the Bushkong tribes of Africa. Despite being neighbours the Bushkong have much higher levels of production and better living standards

ABOVE Butchering and dividing a whale express important aspects of social organization among Alaskan Eskimo (Inupiat) people. A whaling crew cooperates in cutting up a bowhead whale. Whales that are considered a good catch range from 20–60 ft (6–18 m) and provide about 700 lb (320 kg) of usable meat per foot in length. The meat will be distributed to the crews, their families, friends and guests throughout the course of the coming year.

than the Lele. This can be explained by the practice of *polygyny* among the Lele. Lele men are not considered adults with any responsibility for producing food until marriage. The number of women available as wives are in short supply, so men do little productive work until middle age when they have a household of their own to provide for.

REDISTRIBUTION AND EXCHANGE

Anthropologists have also examined systems of redistribution whereby such goods and services pass through networks to people who did not produce them, or who cannot provide them for themselves. If we are to understand the systems of exchange of non-western societies we have to think about the social relations which underpin and influence the nature of economic transactions.

THE GIFT AND EXCHANGE

Marcel Mauss, the French sociologist (1872–1950), examined gift-giving in non-western cultures and argued that its essential nature might be easily misunderstood. His point was that the gift expresses and cements a social relationship, it does not simply transfer ownership of an object from one person to another. In other words, the thing that is given is a symbol of a social relationship between the giver and the recipient of the gift. The gift therefore has value and meaning beyond its material worth.

THE KULA RING

Malinowski's account of a system of exchange and trade called the *kula* illustrates how the need to give and to reciprocate gifts is at the heart of the Trobriand economy. The Trobriand islands are united by a vast ring of ceremonial exchange several hundred miles wide, although the customs and languages of some islands are quite different. People exchange ceremonial objects around this ring and within each island.

There are two kinds of ceremonial objects and each is exchanged around the ring of islands in a different direction. Long necklaces of shells called *soulava* move clockwise. *Mwali,* white armshells, travel anti-clockwise. Mr X publicly and ceremonially presents Mr Y, his 'partner', with a necklace. Mr Y is then obliged to return an equally valuable armshell in the future. The

RIGHT *The division of the catch. As the whale is butchered, the wife of the whaling captain directs the division of the meat into shares which are carefully laid out on the ice. Each crew receives a specific portion depending on their contribution to the catch. As is common among peoples who depend on the sea for their livelihood, individual members of each crew earn a portion of the catch rather than any fixed wage.*

relationship of Mr X and Mr Y as partners is lifelong, maintained by the periodic exchange of objects. Each man usually has a number of *kula* partners both at home and overseas. At home his partners are mainly friends and in-laws and their exchanges are part of a relationship entailing different types of exchange and assistance.

It is also important to note that trade accompanies the *kula*. When canoes set off on their long journeys they are loaded with goods desired by other islanders. However Malinowski stresses that this trade is secondary and the *kula* is the main objective of the journey. Trobriands themselves distinguish *kula* exchanges from the exchange of 'ordinary' goods (*gimwali*). In *gimwali* it is acceptable for people to haggle for advantage openly. An interesting point is that *kula* partners do not engage in *gimwali*, and thus avoid the potential conflict involved in bartering or haggling.

A man will also engage in *kula* (exchange *vaygu'a*) with some important high-ranking social leaders. These men acquire and reinforce their prestige by the number of *kula* partners and the importance of the valuables which pass through their hands. All men strive to maintain a reputation as a generous partner. The more important and numerous the valuables he exchanges the greater his prestige. This means

ABOVE *Nalukataq (blanket toss) is held to celebrate the end of a successful whaling season among Inupiat peoples. At this time all comers are invited to share a large variety of hunted foods, the most important of which is the meat and maktak (black skin and blubber) of the whale. Afterwards people are tossed on a 'blanket' made of walrus or bearded seal skin which acts as a trampoline as a circle of people pull it tight.*

ABOVE *Vegetable vendors at a street market in Jaisalmer, India.*

that he must give generously and obtain strategically at the same time: he cannot do one without the other.

The *kula* expresses the central values of Trobriand society and the economy which is embedded in it. Possession, use and what might be called enjoyment of valuable items take the place of absolute ownership. It is significant that whereas our own valuables tend to be locked away, Trobriand valuables must circulate; they cannot remain as static objects in one person's possession or they will cease to have value. Malinowski did, however, compare *kula* objects with the English Crown Jewels which he saw after completing his field work. He was particularly intrigued when the museum curator talked about the various kings and queens who had worn the jewels, and he recalled the 'personal histories' of *kula* objects and how they are associated with past exchanges and partnerships.

At the same time it is vital to avoid attaching a romantic image to such systems where giving seems more important than keeping. An anthropological account of western economic behaviour might just as easily and erroneously give the impression that people are incapable of generosity or sharing in western society. Malinowski's account makes it clear that the Trobriands, like everyone else, are not immune to hostility, greed and meanness. But what is the meaning of this activity? Some simple answers lie in important aspects of the *kula*. First, the exchanges create relationships of obligation to give and to receive. Second, the partnerships reflect basic elements of political and social life. A man has a limited number of *kula* partners, but whereas a commoner may only have a few, a big chief may have hundreds. Kula partners can live nearby as well as overseas. For the 'average man' local partners may include a village leader and lineage members where bonds of mutual support and assistance are reinforced through *kula* exchanges. Overseas relationships are just as important since they entail protection and hospitality for the traveller who is far from home.

LEFT *Trobriand islanders in the Kula canoes which are used for the 'overseas Kula' when men travel around the ring of islands exchanging highly valued ceremonial objects.*

RELATIONS OF RECIPROCITY

We have considered the debate about the differences between the 'rational', 'economic' motives typified by market behaviour of western society and the supposedly 'irrational, non-material' motives of the non-western world. The work of Marshall Sahlins is interesting in that he does not oppose an impersonal western type of economic activity to a communal face-to-face system of primitive exchange. Following the path trod by Malinowski and Polanyi, Sahlins shows that both types of activity occur in so-called 'primitive' societies. Sahlins described different patterns of reciprocity in terms of a spectrum which ranges from the gift given without expectation of return, to exploitative exchanges.

These forms of reciprocity are contained in many familiar situations. The situation of a child asking for money to buy a parent's birthday present is a good example since it highlights the difference between giving as the expression of a relationship and the mere expenditure of

ABOVE *Street children and beggars form part of the alternative 'black economy' throughout the developing world.*

cash. *Balanced* reciprocity is close to the western idea of the 'economic'. The relationship involved depends upon the obligation to return a gift of equal value and importance. One example can be taken from bar behaviour. The relationships between people buying drinks are likely to be questioned if one person orders cocktails when companions are drinking water. Negative reciprocity is the most impersonal type of exchange. In Sahlins' description 'the participants confront each other as opposed interests, each looking to maximise utility at the other's expense'. A vital point is that even in the most exploitative case of negative reciprocity the 'exploiter' wants to maintain the relationship with the 'exploited'. A trader who engages in 'shady deals' knows he or she cannot go too far, too often, with any one party or he or she will destroy his or her range of customers.

Sahlins is careful to point out that all types of transactions may be found in any particular set of relationships. There is also the issue of how the reciprocity is viewed by the parties concerned. For instance, is there a difference between a business 'bonus/incentive' and the 'gifts' which feature in corruption cases?

AN ECONOMIC NO-MAN'S LAND?

Another complicated situation in economic behaviour occurs where a community is involved in a variety of economic 'spheres' at the same time. For instance people may grow food for their own use and also produce goods they sell to markets for cash. What have become known as peasant economies are typically in this economic 'no-man's-land'. Unlike members of a western market economy or hunter-gatherers, peasants are not totally immersed in one general type of activity. For example some land might not be owned individually, but left aside for communal use.

Allen Johnston's study of a peasant economy in north-east Brazil found a very low level of profit-oriented activity. He was interested in the peasant's motives for concentrating on food rather than cash crops. Two basic options, or

production strategies were identified. One produced a low-yield but had a high level of security for the peasant, the other had a high-yield but low-security. The study showed that the peasants were in a very uncertain and insecure situation. The risks involved in concentrating on production for the markets were considered too great, while a mix of cash crops and food crops produced the least dangers of failure and starvation, if least opportunity for profit. At the national level, peasant economies are also influenced by market forces. This instance of peasant economic activity can be seen as an adaptation to the peripheral position the community occupied in the wider market economy.

A central theme in this exploration of economic anthropology has been the differences and similarities of western, large-scale and small-scale, 'primitive' economies. From the western perspective the term 'economics' tends to denote an area of life which is cut off from everyday social affairs. But, when the economic content of our own social relationships is considered the differences may be less striking than the similarities. Perhaps the essential contribution that anthropologists have made to an understanding of economic activity is that, first and foremost, it is a product of groups and individuals. In Sahlins' terms the economy is 'a function of a society, not a different part'.

ABOVE *The six children of a Caboclo family in the peasant community of Nogueira, Amazonia. A large family represents a valuable labour resource for agricultural work in the fields and gardens.*

ABOVE *As well as a place of prayer and worship, the mosque is an important meeting place, representing both the social and religious centre of the community.*

SOCIETY AND THE SACRED: THE ANTHROPOLOGY OF RELIGION

An anthropologist must try to represent the lives of others as sympathetically and sensitively as possible, no matter what his or her personal customs or convictions may be. This task is perhaps especially difficult in the area of religion. When we enter the realms of belief and symbolism we are studying those parts of a culture that cannot be quantified or reduced to single levels of interpretation. Some anthropologists, like Evans-Pritchard, believed that in order to understand the religion of others, one needed to possess faith oneself. This point of view was perhaps a little extreme, however. As Brian Morris puts it in the introduction to his survey of anthropological studies of religion:

'. . . as an atheist . . . I have tried to follow in my studies the approach that Bertrand Russell advocated with respect to philosophy, namely that the right attitude is neither one of reverence nor contempt, but rather an attitude of critical sympathy' (1987:4).

In the western world, many people have become used to the idea of religion as an declining force. Secularism and science are often believed to be irrepressible forces of industrial society. By way of contrast, non-western peoples have often been represented in films and literature as irrational, obsessed with exotic beliefs or strange rituals.

In fact, both of these images are misleading. Although levels of public worship have declined in the West, this has not necessarily meant that religious belief has disappeared. Often, it is merely 'privatized', as individuals develop personal and idiosyncratic beliefs that have no particular connection with an established faith. In addition, recent decades have revealed how new or revived religions can attract members. Many of the new religious movements like 'Hare Krishna' or the 'Moonies' (Unification Church) have shown the influence of non-western beliefs, particularly on young people. Studies have shown that those who enter are usually far from brainwashed or ignorant. Frequently, they are highly intelligent people who wish to improve the lives not only of themselves, but also of others.

In many communities, religious beliefs and actions form a greater part of the social fabric of society than they do in our society, where religion is treated mostly as a voluntary, leisure-time activity. While 'World Religions' like Christianity or Islam are concerned with the interpretation of sacred texts and the spreading of faith to others, the religious beliefs of many of the people studied by anthropologists are the product of non-literate cultures. The concern may be less with personal salvation or the finer points of theology than with the pragmatic benefits to be gained from the correct performance of rituals or observance of the correct taboos. However, we should avoid falling into the trap of regarding non-westerners as dominated by ritual or magic. As Douglas writes of the Pygmies of the Ituri forest, studied by Turnbull:

> 'Turnbull . . . draws a picture of pygmies, irreverently mocking solemn Bantu rites into which they have been drawn, uncomprehending the magic for hunting and fertility which their Bantu neighbours offer them, overcome with giggling during Bantu attempts to divine for sorcerers . . .' (1970: 33).

What we can say with certainty is that 're-ligion' of some sort has been present in every living community known to humankind. Tylor believed that its core was a 'belief in spiritual beings' (1871), but even this definition may have been too limited, since it is possible to argue that some religions do not include a notion of a specific spiritual being as such. The American anthropologist Geertz has emphasized

LEFT *Pilgrimage to the Shrine of San Marcos in Casariche, Spain. A religious brotherhood organizes this procession each year on 25th March, when an elaborate image of St Mark is taken from the village church to a hillside shrine by tractor. Members of the brotherhood may dress in stylized 'gypsy' costume, leading the procession on horseback, since most Andalusian festivals started as animal fairs run by Gypsies. Today the wealthy middle classes have taken over such events which combine religious elements with secular feasting, drinking and general celebration.*

RIGHT *The colossal Buddha, 38 ft (11.5 m) high, cut into solid rockface at Awkana, Sri Lanka, dates from the 5th century* AD.

the emotional as well as intellectual aspects of religion in stating that religion is:

'a system of symbols which acts to estab-lish powerful, pervasive and long-lasting moods and motivations in men by formu-lating concepts of a general order of exis-tence, and clothing these conceptions with such an aura of factuality that the moods and motivations seem uniquely realistic' (1966: 4).

Of course, religion not only involves beliefs, but also the carrying out of rituals or practices that demonstrate adherence to a faith or respect for a deity. These may include sacrifice, absti-nence from food or eating special foods, and so on.

In the 19th century, cultural evolutionists were generally concerned with the origins of religion and its role in the development of humankind. Did 'primitives' originally worship many gods (*polytheism*), or did they practice a form of *monotheism,* or belief in a single deity, as the Christian faith claimed to? For Tylor, *ani-mism* was the base on which all other 'higher' religions were founded. This was the idea that natural phenomena were imbued with a variety of spirits. Others looked to *totemism*. In other words, the practice whereby a natural item, such as a plant, animal or rock, served as a cen-tral point around which beliefs and social organization were arranged.

Such speculative concern with origins has become less relevant to anthropologists. Now-adays, they are more interested in the role that religion plays in the daily lives of communities, and its relationship to other aspects of social life. Four areas in particular have proved to be fruitful for research:

1) RELIGION AS A FORM OF EXPLANATION

In the West, we instinctively think of religion as being opposed to science, but is this necessarily so? Some scholars have argued that religion can provide a means of explaining actions and events in the world in ways that have some similarities

to the formation of scientific hypotheses. The most forceful recent proponent of this idea has been Robin Horton, a British anthropologist who has worked much in Africa. He says that religious beliefs are actually like scientific ones in the sense that they set up a limited set of principles by which to explain often puzzling events. A scientist explains the world with ref-erence to the predictable action of material forces: the member of a tribe might refer instead to the actions of a personified being such as a spirit.

ABOVE *A carpenter sells mirrors and charms to ward off the Evil Eye and other harmful spirits from his stall in the western district of Hong Kong.*

93

ABOVE *The Temple Tusker,*
regarded as a sacred beast and
powerful symbol, returns to
the temple at the approach of
sunset in Perahera Kandy.
Sri Lanka.

Some important differences between science and such religion also exist, of course. For a scientist, there should be a correspondence between a given theory and what is observed in reality. If an experiment repeatedly fails to produce an expected result, the scientist should re-evaluate his or her assumptions concerning the ways in which given materials react. However, if a believer carries out a ritual in order to obtain rain from the gods and a drought ensues, this result can be rationalized so that the faith remains unchallenged. For instance, the prayer may not have been carried out correctly, or the gods may be displeased with the supplicant. Although it perhaps places too much faith in the readiness of scientists to reject well-worn theories, Horton's approach is imaginative and thought-provoking.

2) RELIGION AS AN EXPRESSION OF COLLECTIVE LIFE

Influenced by 19th-century scholars like Fustel de Coulanges (1830-89) and Robertson-Smith (1846-1904), the French sociologist Emile Durkheim propounded a theory of religion that has proved to be enormously influential. He saw religion as involving beliefs and practices in relation to 'sacred things', in other words things that were separated from the everyday, mundane world. Such beliefs and practices could unite groups into a 'single moral community'. People can come together for collective rituals in which the individual person goes through an intense and emotional experience. The symbols and ideas of the group thus become imprinted on the consciousness of the participant.

Durkheim's theory might appear fanciful. It does not seem to account for the fact that very different ideas about the meaning of a given ritual can exist, even in the same society. However we cannot deny the role of ritual in bringing people together – both intellectually and emotionally. Victor Turner worked among the Ndembu of Zambia, and produced an important analysis of the way they used symbols in ritual. Turner showed how some important dominant symbols recur in many Ndembu rituals. According to the context, each can represent a variety of important values within Ndembu society.

For instance, the *mudyi* tree is a sapling which exudes a white latex if its bark is scratched. It can be taken to stand for a whole series of ideas or images, all concerned centrally with nourishment and dependence. These include among other things female breasts and their milk, womanhood, childbearing and even the whole of Ndembu society. It is possible to understand that the mudyi tree represents all Ndembu women, as a whole, combined against the men of the tribe. We see how a series of ideas, ranging from the physical to the abstract, can be contained within a single symbol, which forms the centre of group worship. Turner writes:

'Ritual, scholars are coming to see, is precisely a mechanism that periodically converts the obligatory into the desirable . . . . In the action situation of ritual, with its social excitement and directly physiological stimuli, such as singing, dancing, alcohol, incense, and bizarre modes of dress, the ritual symbol, we may perhaps say, effects an interchange between its poles of meaning. Norms and values, on the one hand, become saturated with emotion, while the gross and basic emotions become ennobled through contact with social values' (1967: 30).

LEFT *Ghenghis Khan's mausoleum in Ordos, Inner Mongolia. Ghenghis Khan is revered as the founder and greatest hero of the Mongol nation. Some Ordos Mongols make offerings at the mausoleum to honour and worship the spirit of Ghenghis Khan. A cult has emerged in Ordos, dedicated to honouring his spirit which is believed to watch over the Mongol people.*

3) RELIGION AS A MEANS OF VALIDATING SOCIETY

The work of Durkheim and Turner illustrates how religious symbols can help to produce commitment to society's norms among its members. This function of religion can be seen in another way, of course: as reinforcing and justifying the status quo, and thus proving Marx's famous phrase concerning the 'opium of the people' to have been correct. In looking at the Hawaiian chiefs summarized by Keesing in the second section (on 'Warre' and Order), for instance, we saw how an elite group could justify its exalted position in society through reference to divine forces which, in theory at least, could not be challenged.

Malinowski examined the role of myth, or 'sacred tales' among the Trobrianders. He noted

ABOVE *Huge crowds of people queue up to worship a Shiva Lingum in the city of Patan in the Kathmandu Valley.*

that they could be used to explain the origins of and validate existing institutions. Thus, myths described the origins of clans, the relative ranks of sub-clans, and the rights of people to land. Through reference to a sacred past, the claims of the present could be justified. This role of myth can be seen to work in our society, as well. Consider the following passage:

> 'We observe today not a victory of the party but a celebration of freedom – symbolizing an end as well as a beginning – signifying renewal as well as change. For I have sworn before you and Almighty God the same solemn oath our forbears prescribed nearly a century and three quarters ago . . . /The world is very different now . . . . And yet the same revolutionary beliefs for which our forebears fought are still at issue around the globe – the belief that the rights of man come not from the generosity of the state but from the hand of God.'

This is a passage from President Kennedy's inaugural address, as he accepted the office of the Presidency of the United States. When he gave the speech, he was speaking no longer as a candidate from a particular political party, but as a representative for the whole of his country. In such a situation, we see how he appealed to central symbols and ideas which were broad enough to be shared by the vast majority of Americans, and yet specific enough to form a recognizable part of the semi-mythical past of the American republic. Thus, he associated the present-day with the founders of the country. Although he mentioned God, he conveniently avoided specifying the precise religious affiliation of this deity! The effect was to unite large numbers of people through invoking common ideas, which justified the task about to be undertaken.

Many anthropologists' accounts have also examined the role that ancestors play in the belief-systems of certain peoples. These are often elders who have died: rather than being forgotten or becoming remote from human society,

they are perceived as its moral guardians, quick to anger if the precepts or customs of society are broken or disregarded. Among the Lugbara of East Africa, studied by Middleton, they are said to have the power to heal sicknesses, but can also cause misfortune if angered by the behaviour of their descendants. In this role, they function as the opposite of the figure of the witch, in that they represent ideal morality as opposed to a personification of evil or deviancy.

There are numerous other ways in which religious imagery and beliefs can help to justify the political or social mainstream of society. Anthropologists have noted how initiation rituals, for instance, serve to demonstrate and validate the succession of people to a new role

or status. Following the work of Arnold van Gennep (1909), they have noted how these rituals often follow a common structure:

– the separation of the person or group from ordinary life;
– a period of seclusion;
– then the reincorporation of the person or persons into the world with a new status.

The ritual thus separates off the old world (and the old status) from the new period of existence. Initiation may involve such things as the process of transforming young people into socially recognized adults, the recognition of a new chief, or the acceptance of a person into a secret society.

ABOVE *The combination of legal, ritual and personal aspects of marriage. A bride at a Christian wedding makes her thumb-print signature on the official marriage register in Cuzco, Peru.*

97

ABOVE *A female initiation
ceremony among the
Mehinacu people of
Amazonia. Preparation for
initiation into womanhood
involves six months seclusion
in the menstruation hut at the
onset of puberty. The girl
with much paler skin and long
fringe has completed her time
in isolation.*

4) RELIGION AS A FORCE FOR PROTEST AND CHANGE

We have seen that religion can unite people in a community through the sharing of general values or ritual acts that avoid the expression of controversial opinions. However, religion can be just as effective as a force for mobilizing people in the search for change or protest against the prevailing order. Here people are again united – but in a group that comes together in opposition to others.

Max Weber (1864–1920), the German sociologist, made a distinction between the role of the priest and the prophet in religious life which has proved useful. The priest can be seen as part of a stable religious institution. He or she derives authority through knowledge of sacred texts or rituals, and often, as among the Brahmin priests of India, inherits the status of religious specialist. A prophet, on the other hand, is likely to derive authority from claiming a personal relationship with God. Instead of stressing the importance of tradition, he or she will claim to have a special message, or revelation, that is relevant to the particular demands of the day. Through their actions or ethical principles, prophets can

defy orthodoxy and set up a new religious order.

Thus, we can even see Jesus as a form of prophet. Reacting against the Pharisees of the Jewish faith, he stressed a new form of revelation, derived from his position as the Son of God. As so often happens when a prophet begins to gather large groups of people, he encountered resistance from elite groups, concerned about possible challenges to their authority. However, in the long run, the principles of his faith were recorded by disciples and later writers, and became the basis for a new religion which has by now become a tradition in its own right.

Anthropologists have noted that religious movements of protest have often occurred in situations of colonization. These may be concerned with 'revitalization' – the conscious attempt to renew or restore a culture that is seen to be threatened. One means of doing this is to proclaim a 'millennium'. Strictly speaking, this refers to a period of a thousand years, particularly that period when Christ will reign on a prosperous and happy earth, but it has come to mean more generally a vision of the future which can actually be realized through throwing off the yoke of oppression. Thus, in the 19th century, Ghost Dances emerged among American Indian tribes as white settlers moved ever westward, and land and buffalo became increasingly scarce. Led by prophets, these involved dancing rituals and the promotion of visions aimed at the removal of the white man and the return of land and resources to Indians, aided by their ancestors.

Cargo cults in Melanesia represent a slightly different kind of movement. They have tended to occur in areas where native inhabitants have had much contact with westerners, who have come to the area as colonizers and plantation owners. People have felt themselves to be denied the power and the wealth of whites, and apparently lack the means of gaining these. Rather than overtly rejecting western ways, they have sought to adopt new cultural patterns as well as adapting established customs. Thus, often led by prophets, they have chosen to wear

LEFT *An Indian Holy Man.*

RIGHT *A Trobriand islander with an imported plastic container of salt – an innovation in traditional food preparation.*

western clothes or perhaps build air strips, waiting for goods to be flown in. The hope is that by imitating some of the ways of their colonizers, they can obtain the latters' power and wealth for themselves. Some scholars, like the British anthropologist Peter Worsley, have emphasized that the uniting of groups of otherwise separated people has been an important result of these cults. In some circumstances,

they have been converted into effective movements of political protest.

VARIED PERSPECTIVES

Through looking at four aspects of religion, we have begun to perceive its fascinating variety. It can be seen as conservative or revolutionary, intellectual or emotional, personal or collective. These ways of seeing religion can of course be combined to produce a rich analysis of a given case. This can be illustrated with one example, that of the *sar cult*.

IM Lewis has described the pastoral Somali of north-east Africa. They are Muslims, and public worship, politics and wealth are controlled by men. Women have no access to the ownership of camels, a prime source of wealth. They are also expected to be weak and submissive to their husbands.

A number of people can be possessed by *sar spirits,* which are malevolent sprites over which the person has initially no control. They are hungry for food, as well as luxuries, and are often diagnosed as the cause of a wide range of illnesses. A common victim is a married woman whose husband is about to take a second wife, or who feels neglected by her spouse. Through possession, Lewis suggests, women can draw attention to themselves in a society where other means of self expression scarcely exist. Husbands may feel sceptical about the authenticity of possession, but they are often ambivalent, believing in the existence of sar spirits.

We can see how the cult can be viewed from a number of different standpoints. In one sense, it provides a means of explanation for illness. It can also be seen as a form of protest movement, since women are apparently reacting to situation of oppression or stress caused by their structural powerlessness. Lewis shows that they can use possession as a form of oblique strategy: they cannot challenge men directly, but they can influence the latter by invoking the power of spirits over which they claim to have little or no control. The spirits even provide a means of gaining access to valued resources such as perfume or jewellery.

Although it involves an element of protest, the sar cult does not appear to provide a challenge to the status quo. This is both a strength and a weakness. It means the cult can continue without being harshly repressed, and thus carry on providing a form of catharsis or release for those who take part. Possession can be a dramatic and exciting experience, and regular cult meetings may bring women together in a form of solidarity. However, the cult helps relieve the immediate problem of stress, without attacking the societal conditions in which it is produced. Public life continues to be dominated by males.

WAYS OF SEEING THE WORLD: PERSONALITY, PERCEPTION AND CULTURE

An important question has puzzled scholars and writers for many centuries: how much of what we think, say or do is determined by our *nature* (our physical inheritance), and how much by our *nurture,* (our upbringing and culture)? In other words, are we the equivalent of a blank page when we are born – one that is soon filled by a record of the values and predispositions drummed into us by our upbringing? Or have our characters and ways of seeing the world already been formed in the womb?

ABOVE *Public life tends to be dominated by men in the Arab-Muslim world. In contrast, the female domain is the family home.*

ABOVE *Cultural differences and forces of attraction: a Hawaiian woman and a Samoan with traditional tattoo decorations sunbathe on Waikiki beach.*

If you wandered into the common-room of a university and posed this basic question to people from many disciplines, you would receive a variety of conflicting answers. A psychologist, a geneticist and a sociologist would probably enter into a heated debate, each defending the importance of the insights from their own particular disciplines. Here, we are going to look at some of contributions that anthropologists have made to the debate over the years. Although the approaches described have very different aims and methods, they all tend to revolve around a single issue: To what extent is the way we see and react to the world governed by our particular cultural experiences?

THOUGHT AND LANGUAGE

In the first half of this century, two linguists based in the United States made an important and influential claim. Edward Sapir (1884–1939) and Benjamin Whorf (1897–1941) argued that members of different cultures perceived their social and physical environments in very different ways. This was said to be because language does not merely contain or reflect ideas, but actually shapes perception and thought. As Sapir put it:

'Human beings do not live in the objective world alone, nor alone in the world of social activity as ordinarily understood, but are very much at the mercy of the particular language which has become the medium of the expression for their society. It is quite an illusion to imagine that one adjusts to reality essentially without the use of language and that language is merely an incidental means of solving specific problems of communication or reflection . . . . No two languages are ever sufficiently similar to be considered as representing the same social reality' (1949:162).

Thus, one can compare a European language with that of the Hopi Indians. One then discovers important differences in the way items of the world are classified. For instance, while English has only one word for snow, the Hopi distinguish between three varieties. While English has only one word for water, Hopi has two. It almost appears as though Hopi Indians and English-speakers inhabit different universes.

Although highly suggestive, this theory is hard to demonstrate conclusively. It is clearly very difficult to find any means of examining the thoughts and ideas of others. In addition, Sapir and Whorf perhaps tended to over-stress the differences between the languages or cultures they examined. However, they did promote much valuable work, and in some ways echoed the research of a more recent movement within American anthropology called 'ethnosemantics' or the 'New Ethnography'. This has stressed the need for anthropologists to understand and record 'native' concepts of the universe, as revealed through language.

THE RELATIVITY OF CONCEPTS:
A Study in Time

Sapir and Whorf looked at the way in which social factors such as language possibly had an affect on human thought and perception. Meanwhile, in Britain, Evans-Pritchard's classic study, The Nuer (1940) produced an ethnographically very rich analysis of the relativity of human concepts of time, as well as space. He derived his information from extensive

BELOW LEFT Cross-cultural communications: two Ethiopian guides share a bowl of camel's milk beside a film crew's truck during the making of a documentary in the Danakil Desert.

ABOVE *The harvesting of olives, the time for celebration in the agricultural cycle. Men work in teams of three, one team per tree, in Andalusian Spain. The olives are beaten off the tree with long sticks (*varras*) on to sheeting on the ground below. Women gather up 'stray' olives into baskets, before the harvest is taken for cleaning and sorting.*

way of perceiving the world. Evans-Pritchard showed, however, that the Nuer do not share our abstract conception of time. Rather, their ideas are embedded much more closely to perceptions of events in the natural environment or social world. For instance, the monitoring of *oecological time* is based on such things as the passing of the seasons or the phases of the moon. This method of time reckoning is therefore cyclical, depending on the annual cycles of nature.

Although the Nuer have words for today, tomorrow, etc, they do not use these in an exact way. Thus:

> 'When Nuer wish to define the occurrence of an event several days in advance, such as a dance or a wedding, they do so by reference to the phases of the moon: new moon, its waxing, full moon, its waning, and the brightness of its second quarter. When they wish to be precise they state on which night of the waxing or waning an event will take place . . .' (1940: 101).

In industrialized societies, we refer to particular events by using exact terms for days, months and years. To the Nuer, however, it is much more important to think in terms of the spacing between activities. Rather than using the names of months or days to indicate the time of an event, they refer to some important activity in progress during its occurrence, such as the time of early camps, the time of harvesting, and so on. Furthermore, they do not slavishly follow any exact measurement of the passage of seasons or hours in deciding when a task should be performed. As Kuper puts it:

> 'The rainy season, or season of village life, is called *tot*. But the Nuer do not say, it is *tot,* therefore we must move to the upland villages; rather, they say we are in the villages, therefore it is *tot*' (1973: 112).

Similarly, on a daily basis their timepiece is the round of pastoral tasks, rather than any abstract notion of the passing hours. Instead of using the points of the sun across the heavens to

participant observation of this tribal group, based in the Sudan.

We are used to thinking of time as something objective and yet also abstract. It can be divided into units that can be measured on a mechanical timepiece, and these units – whether they are seconds, minutes, hours, etc – remain of the same duration year in and year out. Thus we can arrange to meet at a future time in the full knowledge that we can synchronize our actions. We can also 'waste' time as if it were a concrete resource to be hoarded. It is this attitude which is highly characteristic of an industrialized society, in which the coordination of people and machines is of paramount importance, although, of course, we do have many other views of time as well.

Such a view of time is so central to our behaviour and thought that we are perhaps tempted to think of it as natural – a universal coordinate events, a person may say: 'I shall return at milking', or 'I shall start when the calves come home'.

'*Structural' time,* on the other hand, deals not so much with the Nuers' relationship to nature, but with the interaction of social groups, as well as the life-cycle of the individual person. Thus, it is concerned with births, marriages and deaths, or particular events that have occurred such as weddings, the initiation of age-sets (as described in Section Two), or fights. Since time is seen as involving an order of events of outstanding significance to a particular group, each group will have its own points of reference.

This becomes clear if we examine the names given to years by different tribes. These are floods, famines, wars, and so on, that the particular tribe has experienced – concrete occurrences that are uniqely shared by its members, rather than abstract and universally applicable dates. Perhaps in a similar way we sometimes talk about events 'before the war', or 'after the Great Depression', referring to widely-known aspects of the recent past of for instance, Britain or America.

In our literate society, we are used to thinking of time as a linear progression: we have records showing the development of society

BELOW *Buddhist prayer wheels, symbolic of the notion of time and the cycle of lives, in a Sherpa village, Nepal.*

ABOVE *Young members of the Karamojong tribe pose together in ceremonial costume.*

over hundreds and thousands of years. For the Nuer, who lack such records, history in effect ends a century earlier than the present, and beyond this lie the notions of tradition or myth. Evans-Pritchard writes:

'How shallow is Nuer time may be judged from the fact that the tree under which mankind came into being was still standing in Western Nuerland a few years ago!' (1940: 108).

THE RELATIVITY OF PERSONALITY:
Benedict and Mead

Although adopting rather different methods of study, Evans-Pritchard shared with Sapir and Whorf a concern for the way the members of a

society would classify the world in ways that were culturally-bound and therefore in some sense unique. From the 1920s on, a group of American anthropologists approached the question of *cultural relativity* from a slightly different angle. They were primarily concerned with the relationship between the characteristics of a culture and the personality of its members.

Thus, Ruth Benedict, a student of Boas, carried out research among North American Indians. In 1934 she published a classic book, *Patterns of Culture*. For her, culture could be seen as a larger version of the individual personality. Every culture could be seen as a unique, integrated whole, in which all the basic institutions contributed to a particular pattern or 'configuration'.

Her argument can be illustrated by looking at the way she contrasted two Indian peoples. The

Zuñi of the south-west appeared to be cooperative and moderate in all areas of life. From childhood, people were encouraged to suppress individualistic feelings, and as a result few adults were concerned to contest for positions of leadership. Instead, *collectivism* was valued. Ceremonies lacked any element of trial or ordeal. Using vocabulary derived from the philosopher Nietzsche, she characterized the particular cultural pattern of the Zuñi as *Apollonian*.

In contrast, the Kwakiutl of the north-west could be called *Dionysian*. Unlike the placid Zuñi, they were a frenzied, ambitious, aggressive and highly individualistic people, and such values were instilled by child-rearing techniques which emphasized the individual over the group.

Meanwhile, another student of Boas, Margaret Mead, journeyed to Samoa, and produced work that was to make her famous far beyond the confined boundaries of the academic world. She noted how Samoan children grew up in an atmosphere of very little social or sexual tension, in a society that was characterized by harmony and tolerance. The passage from childhood to adulthood was smooth. This situation clearly contrasted with the often stormy and difficult periods of adolescence of American teenagers.

Mead argued that the problems of puberty could be related to the fact that American society makes the path to maturity as difficult as possible. Thus, social factors were important, and not simply the fact that the person was undergoing considerable physical changes. The individual was required to make sudden leaps in status and responsibility, and by stressing the difference between the adult and the child, Americans were causing rather than identifying the problems of adolescence.

Both Mead and Benedict made the important point that the socialization of the individual provided him or her with many ways of viewing the world and even aspects of personality. They showed how an examination of the influence of childhood experiences could explain much about a person's character. However, their work was rather impressionistic in nature.

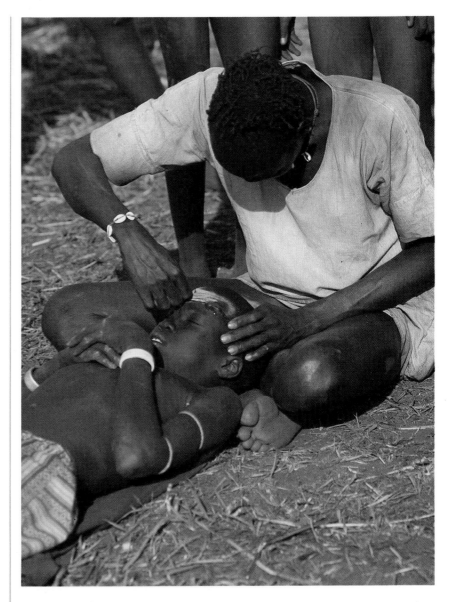

ABOVE *A young girl from the Dinka tribe during the Gornum initiation ceremony, when tribal markings are cut into the forehead. Red ochre will be rubbed into the cuts to prevent infection.*

107

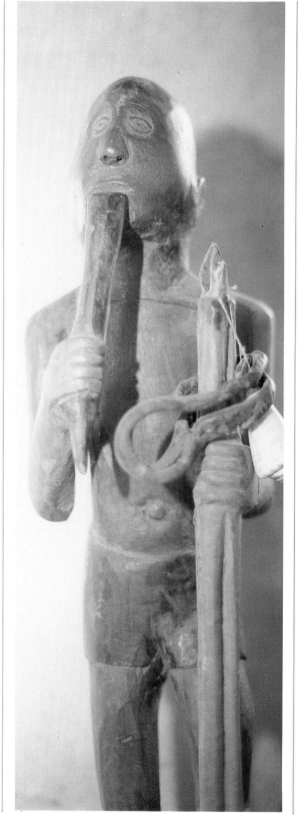

RIGHT *A representation of a male figure. A wooden carving by a Tonga craftsman from the Gwembe Valley, Zambia.*

There is no doubt that Benedict over-stressed the role of culture as an overwhelming force in determining personality, and did not concentrate enough on individual variations. The accuracy of Mead's description of Samoan society has also been the subject of some debate.

THE UNIVERSAL CHARACTERISTICS OF THE MIND?

None of the authors mentioned above would have denied that human beings share important physical characteristics. However, they chose to stress the way culture determines important aspects of human thought and action. Since the Second World War, a rather different view has emerged, championed by a Belgian-born anthropologist based in Paris, Claude Lévi-Strauss. For reasons that will become apparent, this has been termed *structuralism*.

The work is often complex, and only some of its arguments can be discussed here. In a sense, it goes against the idea of cultural relativity by suggesting that human culture is ultimately the expression of the underlying characteristics or structures of the human mind. Although our own society has become technically very specialized and has developed highly abstract forms of logic such as mathematics, all minds and therefore thought processes are basically alike throughout the world.

Humans impose a logical order on the environment, and this is reflected in their ways of classifying the world. Human thought works partly by constructing *binary oppositions:* these might include good versus evil, male versus female, nature versus culture, dark versus light. In other words, the world is divided into contrastive pairs, in a way analogous to the workings of a computer. There is a sense in which any half of an opposition only derives its full meaning from the other half: after all, how can we understand the concepts of light, or good, unless we know what we mean by dark, or evil? Different societies may divide the world up in different ways, but interestingly all seem to use 'oppositions', and some of these are very

ABOVE *A varzea in
Amazonia in the wet season.
Varzea are regions which
are seasonally flooded by
white-water rivers. Homes
are built on stilts and during
the floods people move from
house to house by canoe.*

basic indeed. Which society, for instance, exists which does not distinguish between insiders and outsiders?

Thus, the structures that Lévi-Strauss is searching for lie behind what can be clearly measured or observed. In many ways, his writings seem obscure. He appears to reduce the huge variety of human experience to algebraic patterns produced by the mind that have little to do with important aspects of life such as emotion, or intimate social interaction.

However, many have found his writings use-ful if flawed, and have applied some of his in-sights in examining the way humans classify the world around them. Mary Douglas, the British anthropologist, agrees that humans need to impose a logical order on the universe, though of course the ideas lying behind such an order are inherited across the generations. As members of a given culture, we learn rules about what is generally acceptable and what is not. By following the rules, we accept the authority of society. When they are violated, we feel threatened and discomfited. To illustrate

ABOVE *Aboriginal cave
painting from Mount
Grenfell, New South Wales,
Australia.*

what she means, Douglas looks at the way dirt is perceived in our society. She says that it is, in effect, matter which is out of place, and therefore offending against our ideas of where it should be. Thus:

> 'Shoes are not dirty in themselves, but it is dirty to place them on the dining-table; food is not dirty in itself, but it is dirty to leave cooking utensils in the bedroom, or food bespattered on clothing; similarly, bathroom equipment in the drawing-room; clothes lying on chairs; out-door things in-doors; upstairs things downstairs; under-clothing appearing where over-clothing should be, and so on. In short, our pollution behaviour is the reaction which condemns any object or idea likely to confuse or contradict cherished classifications' (1966: 48).

Like Lévi-Strauss, Douglas accepts that binary oppositions are important: for instance between chaos and order, impurity and purity. She is especially interested, however, in what happens when these distinctions are violated, and anger or unease results. She shows that the way we classify the world has a moral dimension: our outrage at seeing shoes on a table is not simply a matter of medical hygiene, it concerns our deeply-felt adherence to the dictum: 'Everything in its place, and a place for everything'.

In case we wish to argue that the notions of dirt described above are 'natural' or 'objective' in any way, it is worth examining the work of Judith Okely, an anthropologist who has carried out a study of Gypsies in Britain (1983). She shows how Gypsies are concerned to maintain an independent culture, but are also economically dependent on work given by the members of conventional society, whom they call *Gorgios*.

According to the standards of Gorgios, Gypsies appear to be very dirty. Camps are surrounded by rubbish, and display little obvious order, unlike the neat rows of a suburban avenue. Appearances, however, can be deceptive, especially if we take the view of an outsider. Okely shows that Gypsies in fact have very complex and detailed notions of purity and cleanliness. These are different from our own, and there is a sense in which Gypsies feel themselves to be united by their own beliefs, in opposition to a misunderstanding and threatening world. These beliefs apply to commonplace practices such as eating, washing, the use of space or the placing of objects.

Thus, Gypsies make a fundamental distinction between the inside and the outside of the body. The outer shell constitutes the 'public' self, – the one that is forced by necessity to interact with Gorgios. In contrast, the inside must be kept pure and inviolate, and in a sense symbolizes the private, ethnic identity of the independent Gypsy. Any food taken into the body must be ritually clean, and the sharing of eating places with Gorgios is seen as polluting. Just as the body is made up of an internal purity and an external shell, so the inside of a trailer can be distinguished from its outside. Activities considered impure such as clothes washing or defecation must be carried out some distance away. Gypsies therefore consider the Gorgio practice of having toilets inside their homes as extremely polluting!

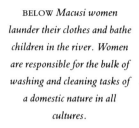

BELOW *Macusi women launder their clothes and bathe children in the river. Women are responsible for the bulk of washing and cleaning tasks of a domestic nature in all cultures.*

RIGHT *A Mongolian couple
in front of a ger (called yurt
in Russian). This portable
dwelling, made of felt, is
ideally suited to the nomadic
lifestyle of peoples from the
Inner Mongolian plains. In
an environment where
temperatures shift from 30°C
to −40°C, the ger provides a
cool environment in summer
and warmth in winter. When
communities move with their
herds to new pastures, the ger
can be disassembled in one
hour and packed on to
wagons.*

We thus see how Gypsies maintain a system of classification, a way of seeing the world, that is in some respects very different from our own. The situation is complicated by the fact that the Gypsies are of course aware of two systems of classification at once: theirs and ours. However, as a group that is constantly threatened by a society which wishes to assimilate them to its ways, their beliefs help to maintain their identity as a bounded group.

If we ask ourselves why we often feel so ambivalent about Gypsies, we might reply that they are dirty, or steal, even if we have never actually met a single 'traveller'. Perhaps, however, we can look at our opinions from a different perspective, aided by the work of Douglas. Is there not a sense in which, to us, Gypsies represent 'matter out of place'? They are a bounded sub-culture that exists not in remote Africa or Asia, but in our very midst. They refuse to accept our bourgeois ideal of the stationary life, controlled by a 'caring' but all-pervasive state. Thus our ambivalence towards them may derive from their lack of fit with our notion of the decent life – a notion which is far from natural or universally shared.

ABOVE Nomadic pastoralists of Inner Mongolia move with their animals in a seasonal cycle; these people are travelling to new pastures from their summer camp.

CHAPTER FIVE

ANTHROPOLOGY IN A

CHANGING WORLD

Iᴛ is becoming increasingly clear that anthropologists have a vital role in increasing our understanding of society *vis-à-vis* socio-economic development and the environment. The second half of this century has been characterized by the retreat of colonialism and the emergence of widespread social, political and economic consequences of the colonial era.

With the issues of overt colonialism largely resolved, in recent decades one of the most important global preoccupations of the industrialized, wealthy nations has been the living standards and quality of life of the poor: the vast majority of the population of the rest of the world. The question is how to solve the problems of poverty and plan for social and economic development.

ANTHROPOLOGY, DEVELOPMENT AND THE ENVIRONMENT

There have been many initiatives applied by the First to the Third World which have brought little advantage to the people being 'developed' or 'aided'. If development schemes are to be successful and operational, they must be suited to local technological and environmental conditions; they must also be appropriate and acceptable to members of the local community. Two extreme examples illustrate the general idea: the installation of a hydro-electric power supply is as inappropiate for a desert settlement as the

exportation of pigs is for a Muslim farming community.

Key words in both cases are 'installation' and 'exportation', for they carry connotations of imposing ideas and activities on a community which may not want outside aid or development in those terms. Development in whose terms and for whose benefit are issues that anthropologists can address.

Fieldwork allows for grassroots opinion to reach the ears of development agencies. Most importantly, the information provided for development projects will incorporate local

ABOVE *An Amazonian Indian quenches her thirst with a city-made import; everyday evidence of the commercial and industrial interests which affect the patterns of life of indigenous peoples.*

OPPOSITE PAGE *A man from the Dogon people of Mali with his highly prized plastic utensils and dishes.*

people's views of their own society, and give details of their customs, culture and way of life. If anthropologists become more involved in development this will allow the perspectives of indigenous peoples to be taken into account. It is also some safeguard against the imposition of misguided or strings-attached solutions which would fail to serve community needs at best, or contribute to new disasters at worst. As more anthropologists from the developing world take the lead in research into problems they have experienced as nationals of their own countries, the situation becomes even more promising for effective and appropriate development activities.

Another key issue is active collaboration with the communities anthropologists are studying. The nature of anthropological fieldwork has always necessitated a high degree of reciprocity

and mutual assistance between the researcher and members of the community. In recent times, given the enormity of problems faced by many communities under study, some anthropologists have opted to make the relations of reciprocity more secure and formal.

One example is the Sacha Runa Foundation which has established a reciprocal arrangement between Ecuadorian forest Indians and anthropologists. A general aim is to help preserve and strengthen the cultural heritage of the native group. As part of this arrangement the Indians receive medical assistance to counteract the effect of introduced diseases, and in return they collaborate in the anthropologists' research projects. The medical services complement traditional medical practices and the programme itself was designed by members of the Indian

RIGHT *Many thousands of indigenous peoples have been killed by diseases and virus infections which were introduced into their regions by contact with outsiders. A western doctor examines a tribal leader during the Altamira meeting of Amazonian Indians.*

community to meet their own needs. In this case, as in other instances of organized collaboration, anthropologists satisfy an obvious self-interest in research goals, but at the same time try to compensate for some of the worst effects of previous western-led invasions of native life.

'There can be no economic interest superior to the necessity of preserving the ecosystem; we do not want a bonanza today at the cost of a desolate future.'

(The words of Carduno, a Mexican Indian leader at the first Congress of the South American Indian Movement, 1980.)

When we consider indigenous peoples' struggles against the dominant forces of modernization and industrialization, it is not difficult to see how the modern world can learn from peoples too often seen as primitive and backward. Many of the same sorts of problems now confronting the international community,

ABOVE *Children displaced by war wearing American T-shirts donated by relief agencies in a Kampuchean refugee camp, Thailand.*

117

BELOW *The devastated landscape, a result of the gold rush and mining in Xingu, close to Altamira, Amazonia.*

from 'lack of natural resources' to 'pollution', have been experienced by minority communities within the frontiers of nation states over the centuries.

The growing realization that unbounded consumerism is not the best or only option, and that other societies are organized on different principles, represents an area where solutions to global concerns may lie for the industrialized world. In a practical sense, traditional, 'primitive' modes of land tenure and production which embody the conservation and sustainability of resources could be applied to tackle the worst excesses of intensive farming and over-production.

These are all subjects which need a higher profile. Where alternative lifestyles and ways of using natural resources are sought, anthropologists are ideally placed to enter the debate with information and analysis of other people's approaches to the environment they inhabit. Steve Rayner (1989) argues that anthropology has been historically concerned with those aspects of human interaction with the environment that are now recognized as crucial by scientists studying global environmental change and the depletion of natural resources.

As well as playing a role in interdisciplinary approaches aimed at providing answers to global environmental research, anthropology can directly contribute to our understanding of environmental issues and increase our capacity to respond to the problem. An understanding of patterns of land-use contributes to our knowledge of the causes of terrestrial and agri- -cultural emissions of 'greenhouse' gases. For example, forest clearing produces carbon di- -oxide emissions while wet rice production and herding are sources of atmospheric methane.

THE POLITICS OF
CONFRONTATION

Drawing on their experience of studies of culturally and geographically isolated societies, some anthropologists, notably Gerlach and Rayner, are offering guides to coordinating and settling disputes derived from different peoples

ABOVE *An area of the Amazonian hinterland which has been settled by incomers. Patches of land in front of the settlers' dwelling have been roughly cleared by fire.*

in a variety of political systems. Throughout the history of contact and conflict between indigenous peoples and new settlers, the original population have struggled to retain control of enough land to ensure their livelihood. The ensuing struggle has always been unequal and the outcome usually at the expense of the weakest groups, the indigenous communities.

In the past, the pattern of confrontation has tended to be eventual compliance in the face of overwhelming odds. In more recent times there has been a shift towards organized opposition, and as in the case of the Indian peoples of the Amazonian rainforest, cooperation between groups facing similar threats to their existence. Communications technology and the flow of reportage to and from the developing world now means that the traditionally weaker side's message filters through to the developed,

industrialized world. The wave of western media attention which threatened to engulf the Kayapo and Yanomami Indians in the summer of 1989 attests to the fact that the old pattern of conflict over the use and control of land may be changing.

The Kayapo Indians initiated the first meeting of Brazil's indigenous peoples of the Amazon to protest against the construction of the Kararão dam. Their leaders announced that they planned to rally to the side of their brothers, the Yanomami. The Yanomami territory, hundreds of miles to the north-west, near the border with Venezuela, was being invaded by gold miners, and was under threat from plans to take three quarters of the land for a national park.

The history of the Amazon's exploitation resonates in the names of tribes now extinct, river tributaries such as Tapajos now fouled

RIGHT *Common perspectives – two sides of the same story. An Indian cameraman focuses on a fellow Kayapo protester, filming alongside a member of a film team, at the opening ceremony of the Altamira meeting of Amazonian Indians.*

LEFT *A Kayapo cameraman
at the Altamira meeting in
Amazonia.*

ABOVE *A Young chief is greeted by the Shaman on returning to his village after negotiations with the government during protests over the construction of the Xingu dam.*

with silt, and long strips of ravaged forest where trees have been felled to make way for roads and pasture land. The tropical forests have been managed and changed by native people for millennia. Orellana, on his 16th century expedition, observed flotillas of canoes and crowds on river banks observing him. By the 20th century most forest dwellers had been driven out or decimated by armed struggle and diseases.

Those who continue to oppose a political economy that favours large land owners and development on a huge scale tend to demand the right to control production and the distribution of 'the fruits of their labour'. The Indian leaders are looking to a redistribution of resources and power, and a development process that incorporates their culture, knowledge and ideas. Hecht and Cockburn describe the largely devastated forest and river banks as 'the consequences of politics and history', and claim that the future of the region and its peoples will be decided by the political forces 'colliding inside Brazil' (1989).

While this is true, international pressure has been useful in buttressing local protests and getting the message across from the perspectives of indigenous groups.

Anthropologists increasingly are involved in monitoring and disseminating information about the plight of indigenous peoples. The traditions of fieldwork and participant observation also make it possible for anthropologists to straddle the boundaries between the cultures in conflict. This kind of mediatory role is both complicated and dangerous since it involves losing supposed 'neutrality'. But the option remains open and some form of active collaboration seems vital in indigenous peoples' struggle for survival.

In an overall academic context where self-examination has revealed past errors, colonialist outlooks and ethnocentrism, critics have called for an accountable anthropology:

'providing on the one hand, the colonised peoples those data and interpretations both about themselves and their colonisers useful for their fight for freedom, and on the other hand, a redefinition of the distorted images of the indigenous communities extant in the national society' (1971, The Barbados Symposium on Interethnic Conflict: The Responsibilities of Anthropology).

At the same time there have been calls for systematic action against practices conducive to *ethnocide,* and for new concepts and explanatory categories which represent local and national reality. Anthropologists have recognized they must adopt a more direct, applied approach and be more than a 'mere verifier of alien theories' (Bodley 1982).

While the call in Malinowski's time was for anthropologists to 'get out of the armchair and into the field', it seems, at the end of the 20th century, that the urgent need is to get out of 'neutral' academia and into the 'front line' in support of 'informants'!

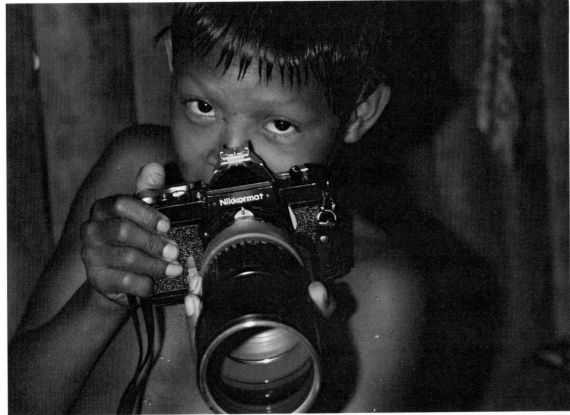

ABOVE *Being accountable for the results of research is of current concern to anthropologists. Members of the Xikru Indians of Amazonia examine a book written about them.*

LEFT *Amazonian Indian child examines an anthropologist's camera. Anthropologists in western societies of the future may look forward to being studied by their former informants.*

GLOSSARY

affines: Relatives by marriage or in-laws.

age-sets: A social category (or corporate group) where membership is based on age. People remain within the same age-set throughout their lives. Each age-set is considered to be more senior as its members grow older.

animism: The belief that natural phenomena are imbued with spirits.

Apollonian: A term derived from the philosopher Nietzsche, used by Ruth Benedict to describe a cultural pattern which is characterized by cooperation and lack of competition. (See also Dionysian.)

balanced reciprocity: A type of exchange relationship which involves the obligation to return a gift of equal value or importance, often after a fixed period of time.

band: A social group composed of people who occupy a common territory and who may hunt and gather food together.

binary oppositions: A two-sided contrast, or juxtaposition of opposites, such as 'good versus evil', which is said by some scholars to reflect a basic feature of the workings of the human mind.

bridewealth: A payment of money and/or gifts from the husband and his family to the bride's family on marriage.

category: A set of things (or people) which are classed together because of certain culturally defined common features.

chiefdom: A form of political organization in which kin groups, public administration and authority are ultimately united under a central figure. The chief may have control of legal and religious affairs and the redistribution of goods.

clan: A descent group where members trace descent from a single ancestor or ancestress but do not know the exact geneological links which connect them to the ancestor or ancestress.

collectivism: A cultural pattern which is characterized by cooperation among members of the community. The individual person is often considered to be of less value than the group.

corporate group: A group of people who act as if they are a legal individual in respect of their collective rights to property, a common name or identity, and other responsibilities.

cultural evolutionism: An analytical approach which considers history as leading towards progressively greater social and cultural complexity.

cultural relativism: An approach to the study of culture whose followers argue that all cultures are unique and are made up of different ideas about the social world. As a result, a culture can only be evaluated and understood in terms of its own standards and values.

descent: A relationship which is defined by people's connection to an ancestor or ancestress through a series of links between one or both parent(s) and child.

Dionysian: A term, derived from the philosopher Nietzsche, used by Ruth Benedict to describe a cultural pattern characterized by aggression, ambition and a stress on the individual over the group. (See also 'Apollonian'.)

dispute settlement: A culturally recognized way of resolving conflicts between members of a community or different groups.

domestic mode of production: An economic system where the bulk of productive tasks are performed by members of the domestic group who live together.

dowry: The money and/or valuables a bride receives from her family on marriage. As part of the marriage agreement the dowry may be transferred to the bride's husband, to his family or to the couple's children. (See also bridewealth.)

endogamy: A marriage rule which requires members of a community to marry partners from within a defined group or kinship category. This is also called 'in-marriage'. (See also Exogamy.)

ethology: The study of animal behaviour in its natural setting.

ethnoarchaeology: The study of the use of everyday items and artefacts in the present in an attempt to discover details of social life in the past.

ethnocentrism: A way of thinking about or describing other cultures based purely on one's own cultural standards, customs and values.

ethnocide: A systematic policy to murder and destroy the culture of all the members of a particular race or social category.

ethnography: The recording and analysis of a particular culture based on field research.

exogamy: A marriage rule which requires people to marry outside a particular group or kinship category. This is also called 'out-marriage'. (See also endogamy.)

faction: A sub-group of members (often discontented) of a larger social group or category.

fictive kinship: A form of social relationship between people who are not related by blood, involving emotional ties and social obligations similar to those expected between blood-relatives.

formalism: A position in economic anthropology which states that western (neoClassical) economic theory can be applied to all human societies. (See also Substantivism.)

genealogy: A way of describing the web of relationships traced through parent-child ties, as in a pedigree.

generalized reciprocity: A type of exchange relationship where participants are often closely related through for instance kinship ties, and where little attempt is made to ensure a perfect balance of the value or quantity of things exchanged.

gimwali: The Trobriand islander's term for trade within the Kula system of exchange.

Gorgios: The word used by Gypsies to refer to people who are not members of the Gypsy community.

hominid: A member of the family of the order primates to which humankind is said to belong.

hunter-gatherers: The members of a society who live in a close relationship with the natural environment, providing food (exclusively or primarily) by collecting wild plants and hunting.

indigenous: Native, with particular reference to the original inhabitants of an area and their way of life.

jural: Relating to a system of law or legal and binding obligations.

key informant: An individual who provides an anthropologist with particularly detailed information as part of a close relationship of mutual trust and understanding. This can provide the anthropologist with very rich material based on the "insider's" view of his or her own social world.

kin group: A social group whose members define their relationship to each other in terms of their common descent or kinship.

kinship: A social relationship which is based on culturally recognized links between parents and children, and which is further extended to brothers and sisters and more distant relatives.

kula: A type of exchange carried out by the Trobriand islanders of Melanesia. Highly valued ceremonial goods are exchanged around the ring of islands, accompanied by trade in other goods.

life histories: Accounts of people's lives and experiences recorded during field research.

lineage: A unilineal descent group whose members trace descent through the male or the female line by known genealogical links from an ancestor or ancestress.

mater: The socially recognized mother of a child. This woman may not be the biological mother.

matrilineal: A principle of descent from an ancestress which is traced in the female line.

maximization: The assumption in economic theory and formalist economic anthropology that people will make decisions rationally, deploying scarce resources in ways that will bring the greatest possible reward.

means of production: In Marxist theory, this refers to the resources people use in production, such as tools, raw materials and technological knowledge.

mechanical solidarity: Emile Durkheim's term for the way society is held together when its members share common skills, customs and beliefs. (See also organic solidarity.)

monogamy: A marriage rule which requires that each member of society has no more than one spouse.

monotheism: The belief in a single, all-powerful god.

moot: An informal hearing of a legal dispute before other members of the community.

mwali: A highly valued armshell. One of the ceremonial objects exchanged in the Trobriand Kula ring.

negative reciprocity: A type of exchange relationship akin to barter, in which social ties between participants are minimal.

norm: An explicit or implicit guide for customary social behaviour.

organic solidarity: Emile Durkheim's term for the way society is held together when its members perform specialized tasks and therefore rely on each other's complementary skills and functions. (See also mechanical solidarity.)

palaeoanthropologist: A scholar interested in the fossil remains of primates.

participant observation: The study of the ways of life of a people or group through living closely with its members, taking part in everyday life and recording behaviour and beliefs.

pater: The socially recognized father of a child, who may not be the biological father.

patrilineal: A principle of descent from an ancestor which is traced in the male line.

polyandry: Marriage of a woman to more than one man.

polygamy: The practice of having more than one spouse.

polygyny: Marriage of a man to more than one woman.

polytheism: Belief in and worship of more than one god. (See also monotheism.)

(pro)genitor: The biological father of a child.

(pro)genitrix: The biological mother of a child.

sanction: Reward for socially approved behaviour (positive sanction), or restraint on deviant behaviour (negative sanction).

structuralism: A theory most commonly associated with Lévi-Strauss, which attempts to find the underlying principles governing the workings of the human mind which also lie behind the structuring of culture and society. (See also binary opposition.)

soulava: A highly valued necklace. One of the ceremonial objects exchanged in the Trobriand Kula ring.

substantivism: A form of economic theory opposed to *formalism*. Substantivists argue that the market-oriented, maximizing models of economic behaviour used by formalists are applicable only in western contexts. The forms of reciprocity and redistribution present in other societies have to be analyzed through using other models.

succession: The taking-over of a vacant office or position.

totemism: The practice whereby a social group, such as a lineage or clan, is associated symbolically with a particular natural item or phenomenon.

unilineal: Descent traced in one line, ie either matrilineal or patrilineal.

BIBLIOGRAPHY OF BOOKS
USED IN TEXT

Barley, N, *The Innocent Anthropologist* (Penguin, 1983, 1986)

Bodley, JH, *Victims of Progress* (Benjamin Cummings Publishing Company, California, 1982)

Benedict, R, *Patterns of Culture* (Mentor, 1934, 1953)

Chagnon, N, *Yanomamö* (Holt, Rinehart & Winston, 1968)

Douglas, M, *Purity and Danger* (Penguin, 1966); *Natural Symbols* (Cresset, 1970)

Evans-Pritchard, EE, *The Nuer* (Clarendon, 1940)

Fortes, M & Evans-Pritchard, EE, *African Political Systems* (Oxford University, 1940)

Fox, R, *Encounter with Anthropology* (Penguin, 1975)

Geertz, C, 'Religion as a Cultural System' (in M Banton, ed, *Anthropological Approaches to the Study of Religion,* Tavistock, 1966); *The Interpretation of Cultures* (Basic Books, 1973)

Hecht S & Cockburn A, *The Fate of the Forest* (Verso, 1989)

Hugh-Jones, S, *The Palm and the Pleiades* (Cambridge University, 1979)

Keesing, R, *Cultural Anthropology* (Holt, Rinehart & Winston, 1976, 1981)

Kuper, A, *Anthropologists and Anthropology* (Allen Lane, 1973)

Lewis, IM, *Social Anthropology in Perspective* (Penguin, 1976, 1981)

Luhrmann, T, *Persuasions of the Witch's Craft* (Blackwell, 1989)

Malinowski, B, *Argonauts of the Western Pacific* (Routledge & Kegan Paul, 1922); *A Diary in the Strict Sense of the Term* (Routledge & Kegan Paul, 1967); *Coral Gardens and Their Magic* (Allen & Unwin, 1935)

Morris, B, *Anthropological Studies of Religion* (Cambridge University, 1987)

Okely, J, *The Traveller-Gypsies* (Cambridge University, 1983)

Pelto, *Anthropological Research* (1970)

Peters, E, Aspects of Bedouin bridewealth in Cyrenaica (in JL Comaroff, ed, *The Meaning of Marriage Payments* London, Academic Press, 1980)

Pryce, K, *Endless Pressure* (London, 1979)

Quiggin, A, *Haddon the Head Hunter* (Cambridge University, 1942)

Radcliffe-Brown, AR, *The Andaman Islanders* (Cambridge University, 1922)

Robbins, L, *The Subject Matter of Economics, an essay on the nature of Economic Science* (Macmillan, 1935)

Sahlins, M, *Stone Age Economics* (Aldine-Atherton, 1972)

Sapir, E, *Selected Writings . . . ,* (D Mandelbaum, ed, University of California, 1949)

Stocking, G, *Victorian Anthropology* (Free Press, 1987)

Strathern, A, *Ongka* (Duckworth, 1979)

Turner, V, *The Forest of Symbols* (Cornell University, 1967)

Tylor, EB, *Primitive Culture* (John Murray, 1871)

Van Gennep, A, *Les Rites de Passage* (The Rites of Passage) (Librairie Critique Emile Nourry, 1909)

Yong, D, 'The Courtroom Performance' (in *Cambridge Anthropology,* 10:3, 1985)

SUGGESTIONS FOR
FURTHER READING

Beattie, J, *Other Cultures* (Cohen & West), 1964)

Bohannan, P & Glazer, M, *High Points in Anthropology* (Alfred A Knopf, New York, (1976)

Cheater, A, *Social Anthropology: An Alternative Introduction* (Unwin Hyman, 1986)

Cohen, AP, *The Symbolic Construction of Community* (Tavistock Publications, 1985)

Donner, F, *Shabono* (Paladin, 1984)

Durkheim, E, *The Elementary Forms of the Religious Life* (Free Press, (1915) 1954)

Fox, R, *Kinship and Marriage* (Penguin, 1967)

Gluckman, M, *Essays on the Ritual of Social Relations* (Manchester University, 1962)

Honigmann, J, *The Development of Anthropological Ideas* (Dorsey, 1979)

Keesing, R, *Kin groups and Social Structure* (Holt, Rinehart & Winston, 1975)

Lessa, W & Vogt, E, *Reader in Comparative Religion* (Harper & Row, 1958 and later editions)

Lévi-Strauss, C, *The Savage Mind* (University of Chicago Press, 1966)

Mair, L, *An Introduction to Social Anthropology* (Clarendon, 1965 and later editions)

Pocock, D, *Understanding Social Anthropology* (Hodder & Stoughton, 1975)

Roberts, S, *Order and Dispute: An Introduction to Legal Anthropology* (Penguin, 1979)

Young, M & Willmott P, *Family and Kinship in East London* (Pelican Books, 1957)

Young, M (ed), *The Ethnography of Malinowski* (Routledge & Kegan Paul, 1979)

PICTURE CREDITS

Barbara Bodenhorn: pages 83, 84 and 85.
Deborah da Lima: pages 15, 39, 77 (top), 81 and 109;
jacket: row 1 picture 2.
CM Dixon: pages 23, 30 (top right), 31 (left), 33
(bottom), 92 and 110.
ET Archive: pages 20, 22 (top), 28 and 33 (top).
Mary Evans Picture Library: pages 10 (left) and 29 (top).
Michael Freeman: jacket: row 1 picture 1, row 3 pic-
tures 2 & 3, row 4 pictures 3 & 4, row 4 pictures 4 &
5, row 5 pictures 1, 3 & 4, back jacket.
GSF Picture Library: pages 21 and 108.
Mario Guarino: pages 17, 91 and 104.
Christine Hugh-Jones: pages 16 (bottom), 116, 120
and 121.
Hutchison Library: 7, 8, 10 (right), 11, 12 (top), 25,
27, 32 (top), 36, 46, 51, 55, 58, 63 (bottom), 64, 66,
67, 70, 72, 98, 105, 114, 122 and 123 (bottom).
T Beddow: page 79.
Dave Brinicombe: page 43.
Sarah Errington: page 53.
Carlos Freire: page 74.
JG Fuller: page 30 (top left) and 93.
Hiridörig, Vision International: page 37 (right).
Michael Mackintyre: pages 34 (top), 42, 45, 73, 100,
102 and 123 (top).
P Montanon: page 99.
P Edward Parker: pages 26 (bottom) and 97.
Jenny Pate: page 86.
W Jesco V Puttkamer: pages 61 (bottom) and 119.

John Ryle: page 75.
Mischa Scorer: page 38.
André Singer: page 87.
Nigel Smith: page 44.
Liba Taylor: page 117.
William MacQuitty: page 63 (top).
*Smithsonian Institution, National Anthropological
Archives:* page 24.
David Sneath: pages 32 (bottom), 56, 61 (top), 76, 95,
112 and 113; jacket: row 1 picture 3, row 2 picture 3.
Survival Anglia Ltd:
    Liz & Tony Bomford: page 16 (top).
    JB Davidson: 26 (top) and 54.
    Richard Kemp: pages 13, 60 and 80.
    Richard & Julia Kemp: page 107.
    Lee Lyon: page 22 (bottom), 40, 41, 69, 78 and
    103.
    Dieter & Mary Plage: page 94.
    Alan Root: pages 50, 49, 62 and 106.
    David Simonson: page 34 (bottom).
    Maurice Tibbles: page 111.
    Bridget Wheeler: page 115.
    Colin Willock: page 77 (bottom).
Declan Quigley: pages 12 (bottom), 19, 29 (bottom),
35, 59, 71 and 96.
Maya Unnithan: pages 6, 18, 31 (right) and 37 (left).
Helen Watson: pages 9, 14, 30 (bottom), 47, 65, 68,
82, 88, 90 and 101.